THE BEST OF

Bible Answers Live

VOLUME 2

with
DOUG BATCHELOR
and
JËAN ROSS

The Best of Bible Answers Live, Vol. 2

Published by Amazing Facts International
P.O. Box 1058
Roseville, CA 95678
800-538-7275 | afbookstore.com

Compiled by Doug Batchelor
Edited by Curtis Rittenour and Laurie Lyon
Cover Design by Daniel Hudgens
Text Layout by Greg Solie • Altamont Graphics

ISBN: 9781580196871

TABLE OF CONTENTS

REAL CHANGE

How much do we actually benefit from keeping
Jesus' principles and commands?

*"He who keeps instruction is in the way of life, but he who
refuses correction goes astray" (Proverbs 10:17).*

Every advice, principle, and command of Jesus provides a
person with outstanding blessings! The biggest lottery winner
in history pales in comparison to God's rich blessings to His
obedient children.

Here are just a few benefits that come from following Jesus' rules:
Jesus as a personal friend; freedom from guilt and fear; peace of mind;
indescribable happiness; better health and a longer life; no hangovers;
assurance of a home in heaven!

Jesus compared the people who are obedient to His words to
someone building on a strong foundation. He said, "Whoever comes
to Me, and hears My sayings and does them, I will show you whom
he is like: He is like a man building a house, who dug deep and laid
the foundation on the rock. And when the flood arose, the stream
beat vehemently against that house, and could not shake it, for it was
founded on the rock" (Luke 6:47, 48). It's not enough to just hear His
words and agree with them; we need to take action and do as He has
asked. We need to live His commands.

Besides those benefits listed above, He promises: "I will never
leave you nor forsake you" (Hebrews 13:5); "I have loved you with an
everlasting love" (Jeremiah 31:3); and "I will strengthen you, yes, I will
help you, I will uphold you with My righteous right hand" (Isaiah 41:10).

Jesus tells us, "To him who overcomes I will give to eat from the tree
of life, which is in the midst of the Paradise of God" (Revelation 2:7).
And what could top this promise? "He who overcomes shall inherit all
things, and I will be his God and he shall be My son" (Revelation 21:7).
In following Jesus, we are adopted into His family. As children of God,
we become heirs of everything—the entire universe!

Talk about riches! The true Christian receives benefits from
his heavenly Father that even the richest people on Earth can
never purchase.

SALVATION STEPS

What are the basic steps to becoming a Christian?

"But as many as received Him, to them He gave the right to become children of God, to those who believe in His name" (John 1:12).

The most important step in giving your life to God is to realize how much He loves you. The Lord wants everyone to be saved. God isn't trying to keep people out of heaven. In fact, Jesus came and gave His life for us so that we might receive salvation. "For this is good and acceptable in the sight of God our Savior, who desires all men to be saved and to come to the knowledge of the truth. For there is one God and one Mediator between God and men, the Man Christ Jesus" (1 Timothy 2:3–5).

We must next admit that we are sinners and lost without Jesus. "The heart is deceitful above all things, and desperately wicked; who can know it?" (Jeremiah 17:9). "For all have sinned and fall short of the glory of God" (Romans 3:23). "For the wages of sin is death, but the gift of God is eternal life in Christ Jesus our Lord" (Romans 6:23).

We then repent of our sins. We acknowledge them and turn from them. "Repent therefore and be converted, that your sins may be blotted out" (Acts 3:19). "If we confess our sins, He is faithful and just to forgive us our sins and to cleanse us from all unrighteousness" (1 John 1:9). Then believe God has forgiven you. "In Him we have redemption through His blood, the forgiveness of sins, according to the riches of His graces" (Ephesians 1:7).

Accept God's free gift of salvation. "For by grace you have been saved through faith, and that not of yourselves; it is the gift of God" (Ephesians 2:8). Since you now are a child of God, the Lord will begin to work in your life in amazing ways. "But as many as received Him, to them He gave the right to become children of God, to those who believe in His name" (John 1:12).

THE NEW JERUSALEM

Is the holy city really big enough to hold all the saved people of all ages?

"In My Father's house are many mansions; if it were not so, I would have told you. I go to prepare a place for you. And if I go and prepare a place for you, I will come again and receive you to Myself; that where I am, there you may be also" (John 14:2, 3).

First, let's get a little perspective on the size of New Jerusalem. The Bible says, "The city is laid out as a square; its length is as great as its breadth. And he measured the city with the reed: twelve thousand furlongs. Its length, breadth, and height are equal" (Revelation 21:16). The city is perfectly square. Its perimeter is 12,000 furlongs, or 1,500 miles (a furlong is 1/8 mile). It is 375 miles long on each side. That equals more than 140,000 square miles, a little bigger than the state of New Mexico!

If the city were to be crowded and each saved person given only 100 square feet of ground space, there would be room for 39 billion people in the city, which is many times larger than the present population of the world. Many statisticians believe that if all the people who have ever lived were saved, there would be plenty of room for them in the city.

When Jesus told His disciples that He would be leaving them, they were troubled. To comfort them, Christ explained that He would be going to His Father's house where there are "many rooms." In addition, He assured them that He was going "to prepare a place" for each of them. It reminds me of kids going to visit their grandparents on a big farm out in the country. The old home is large and has plenty of space for everyone.

The heavenly Father has plenty of room in His place for each of His children. The Creator of the universe is not limited on space. His love knows no bounds!

TEMPTATION

What are some tips on how to handle temptation?

"A prudent man foresees evil and hides himself, but the simple pass on and are punished" (Proverbs 22:3).

There are many suggestions in the Bible for dealing with temptation, but the most important tip is this: Run! Few speed records are broken when people run from temptation. They often crawl away from it hoping it catches up with them. Sometimes temptation comes through a door we deliberately leave open.

Suppose that you accidentally spilled kerosene all over your clothes and somebody nearby lit a match. Where would you go? As far away as you could and as fast as possible! That should be the attitude of a Christian toward temptation. Paul said, "Flee sexual immorality" and "flee from idolatry" (1 Corinthians 6:18; 10:14). So run away from sin, and don't leave a forwarding address.

Don't miss this: When you run from temptation, you head toward God. "Draw near to God and He will draw near to you" (James 4:8). When you know something is sinful, don't engage or banter with the devil, because he is the master of rationalization—that's how Eve fell!

It breaks my heart when Christians try to justify their sins. There is no limit to the arguments with which the devil can supply you. As soon as you know something is wrong, flee! The bravest person runs from temptation; the fool flirts with it.

The most precious way to overcome any temptation has to be because you love God. You know that sin hurts God, and when tempted you need to say out loud, "I can't do that because I love God." The more you love Jesus, the less the attractions of the devil will hold sway over you.

We're all tempted, but the Lord has promised that we can be overcomers through the "exceeding great and precious promises" found in the Scriptures. Jesus will teach us how to overcome. The devil could not make Jesus sin, nor can he make us. "But thanks be to God, who gives us the victory through our Lord Jesus Christ" (1 Corinthians 15:57). Ask Him for overcoming power and joyfully dive into the pages of His Word!

TOTAL SURRENDER

How do I fully surrender my life to God?

"From there you will seek the LORD your God, and you will find Him if you seek Him with all your heart and with all your soul" (Deuteronomy 4:29).

This is the most important question we can ask: How can I know I'm a genuine Christian? How can I know that I'm totally surrendered to God and that I've said, "Lord, my life is yours"? Our text above indicates that in order to find God's will, we need to be looking for Him with everything we've got. This implies complete sincerity. It means that we have gone beyond recognizing our need of God and have put our full effort into seeking Him through His Word and through prayer.

God has given us the power to choose. He won't force His ways on us, but He invites us to "choose for yourselves this day whom you will serve" (Joshua 24:15). The first thing to do is to choose to serve God.

We can then pray, "Lord, I'm willing to follow you." But if you're not sure you're willing but you want to be, you can even pray, "Lord, make me willing to be willing."

What about those times we do things we know we shouldn't? Paul describes this struggle in Romans 7:15: "What I will to do, that I do not practice; but what I hate, that I do." How do we overcome this cycle of sin and get victory over the flesh? Paul says, "I thank God—through Jesus Christ our Lord!" (v. 25). God promises to do that for us by faith in Jesus. We need to yield our will to Christ. Continue to pray and tell God, "I'm willing for You to work in my life and do whatever You need to do."

Finally, don't get discouraged. Remember that surrendering your life to God is not a one-time event; it must be a daily commitment. The apostles followed Jesus for three-and-a-half years before they were fully converted. Our progress happens over time as we trust in Him and stay committed to Him. So it's important to renew that allegiance every day.

SHARING YOUR FAITH

How can I share the truth about God with my friends?

"A friend loves at all times" (Proverbs 17:17).

First, let's discuss what we shouldn't do when sharing our faith: *argue.* People don't respond well to argument. When hearts are proud or stubborn, we dig in and fight—no matter what creative, logical arguments are presented. So don't preach *at* people and don't be arrogant. Remember, you were once in their position (see Ephesians 2:13).

There are three specific things we can do to share God with those we care about:

Be a true friend and listen. Then, if they are open to it, share information. The Bible says, "Let your speech always be with grace, seasoned with salt, that you may know how you ought to answer each one" (Colossians 4:6). It's a good idea to pray, asking the Holy Spirit to guide you and help you know when to speak and what to say. Share with your friends what God has done for you personally. How has a relationship with Him changed your life for the better? That can make a real impact in someone's thinking. Sometimes sharing a book or a DVD works well, especially with people who are argumentative.

Be a good example. You don't want to be un-Christ-like and get angry at your friends if they disagree with you. That's not the way Jesus would win them over. But you can set an example in the way that you live. If love is your motivation in life, people will notice. "In all things [show] yourself to be a pattern of good works; ... [use] sound speech that cannot be condemned, that one who is an opponent may be ashamed, having nothing evil to say of you" (Titus 2:6–8).

Pray for your friends, consistently and patiently. Remember, "The effective, fervent prayer of a righteous man avails much" (James 5:16). We can't see things the way God does, and sometimes it takes months or years for Him to reach those we love. Trust that He wants to save your friends even more than you do. Don't give up. Keep on praying.

Stumbling

If I accept Christ and His forgiveness and then fall again, will He forgive me again?

"A righteous man may fall seven times and rise again, but the wicked shall fall by calamity" (Proverbs 24:16).

The disciple Peter once approached Christ and asked, "Lord, how often shall my brother sin against me, and I forgive him? Up to seven times?" (Matthew 18:21). Some believe the rabbis of his day taught forgiving others three times was sufficient and that Peter was seeking to be generous in how he asked Jesus the question. Christ's response must have caught him off guard: "I do not say to you, up to seven times, but up to seventy times seven" (v. 22).

Most of us would lose count if we tried to remember to forgive people that many times—which is the point of Christ's message. The idea of legalistically trying to count the number of times you should forgive a person takes away the heart of forgiveness. The apostle Paul taught, "Love suffers long" (1 Corinthians 13:4). True forgiveness doesn't keep a tally of offenses.

To illustrate how longsuffering we should be toward others, Jesus tells Peter a story about a servant who was forgiven an enormous debt, but who then turned around and would not forgive someone else a small debt. His master heard what happened and said, "You wicked servant! I forgave you all that debt because you begged me. Should you not also have had compassion on your fellow servant, just as I had pity on you?" (Matthew 18:32, 33).

The point is clear: We should be just as compassionate toward others who fail as God is toward us. The way we relate to others is based on how God treats us. If Jesus says we should be willing to forgive people who have fallen so many times that we cannot even keep track, is the heavenly Father any less compassionate when we fail?

The Bible teaches, "If we confess our sins, he is faithful and just to forgive us our sins, and to cleanse us from all unrighteousness" (1 John 1:9). God doesn't put a number on this promise. If we humbly come to Him and genuinely repent, we can know that He hears us and forgives us.

THE ARK OF THE COVENANT

Where is the Ark of the Covenant located today?

"There I will meet with you, and I will speak with you from above the mercy seat, from between the two cherubim which are on the ark of the Testimony" (Exodus 25:22).

After the Exodus, God instructed Moses to build a tabernacle where He would dwell among His people. The tabernacle structure was designed around a sacred centerpiece called the Ark of the Covenant, a rectangular chest set with two statues of angels looking down on top of it, a place called the mercy seat. This ark was placed within the temple's second compartment, the "holy of holies."

Later, King David had the ark transferred to Jerusalem, and Solomon, his son, placed it in the midst of a spectacular temple he had built. Originally, the ark only contained the two stone tablets of the Decalogue. Later, Aaron's rod and a small pot of manna were also placed inside; the book of the law was put in the side of the ark (see Exodus 25:21; Deuteronomy 10:3, 5; and Exodus 16:33, 34).

The last time the ark is mentioned is in 2 Chronicles 35:3, during the reign of King Josiah. Naturally, many have wondered where this special chest now resides. Since the time Nebuchadnezzar destroyed Jerusalem, the Bible makes no mention of where the ark went. The Scriptures itemize many other vessels that were captured by the Babylonians, but the ark itself is clearly missing.

Based on 2 Maccabees 2:4–8, some believe the prophet Jeremiah was instructed by God to move the ark outside Jerusalem before the city was destroyed and to hide it in a cave on Mount Nebo. This seems unlikely because at this same time, the Babylonian king had Jerusalem completely surrounded. It is more reasonable to assume that Jeremiah, with the help of loyal priests, hid the golden ark in one of the many caves or tunnels that honeycomb the ancient city of Jerusalem. To this day, the ark's location remains one of archeology's greatest secrets.

But what really matters most is that the law of God is hidden within our hearts. Finding the ark will not matter if we do not have the law within.

TRUTH

How can I really know truth?

"You shall know the truth, and the truth shall make you free"
(John 8:32).

When people ask me this question, they are typically not wondering about the latest scandal in the tabloids (which are mostly far-removed from truth). They are seeking answers to life's big questions and are looking to understand divine things.

The Bible is clear that the ultimate source of truth comes from God. The Scriptures explain this in more than one way. "Jesus said to him, 'I am the way, the truth, and the life. No one comes to the Father except through Me'" (John 14:6). The Holy Spirit is also a provider of truth. "It is the Spirit who bears witness, because the Spirit is truth" (1 John 5:6). So also God's Word, the Bible, is a foundation of truth: "Sanctify them by Your truth. Your word is truth" (John 17:17).

One of the principles for finding God's truth is that we must be earnest in our search. "You will seek Me and find Me, when you search for Me with all your heart" (Jeremiah 29:13). We should also pray for God to guide us to truth. "However, when He, the Spirit of truth, has come, He will guide you into all truth" (John 16:13).

Some people are not willing to give up cherished ideas when they are looking for truth. The Bible warns, "There is a way that seems right to a man, but its end is the way of death" (Proverbs 14:12). We must be humble and open to truth. "Cease listening to instruction, my son, and you will stray from the words of knowledge" (Proverbs 19:27).

If you are studying a Bible passage that stumps you, pray for God to give you understanding, and then search other verses on the topic. Use a concordance and compare Scripture with Scripture. "For precept must be upon precept, precept upon precept, line upon line, line upon line, here a little, there a little" (Isaiah 28:10).

Most of all, search the Scriptures and look for Jesus. It is through God's Word that we most clearly see the Source of all truth.

BOOKS OF THE BIBLE

How were the books of the Bible chosen?

"The words of the LORD are pure words, like silver tried in a furnace of earth, purified seven times.... O LORD, You shall preserve them from this generation forever" (Psalm 12:6, 7).

The Bible is made up of 66 books, written by approximately 40 authors over a period of 1,500 years. The word "canon" means "measuring rod," and it's the word that describes the standard version of Scriptures we have today. The careful process of determining which books would make up the Christian Bible occurred in the early church.

The earliest indications of Old Testament canon come from the time of Ezra and Nehemiah during the Babylonian captivity (605–535 B.C.). But the process was probably not complete until sometime around 200 BC. Deciding which books to include was done by senior priests based on general agreement that each book was authentic and divinely inspired.

The Old Testament is not greatly disputed and is generally the same for both Protestants and Jews. These writings are repeatedly affirmed and quoted at least 400 times in the New Testament by Jesus and others!

We know more about development of the New Testament. The majority of these 27 books were recognized as inspired within 50 years of the death of the apostle John. By careful, prayerful evaluation, the early church reviewed the best nominees to include. They began by choosing books that were endorsed by the apostles. For example, Peter recognized Paul's writings as Scripture (2 Peter 3:15, 16).

The first New Testament "canon" was the Muratorian Canon, compiled in AD 170. It included everything but Hebrews, James, and 3 John. Then in AD 363, the Council of Laodicea affirmed all 27 books were to be read in the church. Later councils within the next 50 years also affirmed the same 27 books as authoritative.

The history of this process demonstrates that God's hand was leading all along the way. The church recognized and received by faith documents that had the obvious mark of divine inspiration. An unbiased study of all the different pieces of literature from this time will affirm the clear mark of the true Word of God.

IGNORANCE AND SALVATION

What will happen to people who have never heard about Jesus?

"That was the true Light which gives light to every man coming into the world" (John 1:9).

The apostle Paul dealt with this question when writing to the church at Rome. In speaking of the light of the law as clearly given in the Old Testament, he says, "For as many as have sinned without law will also perish without law, and as many as have sinned in the law will be judged by the law" (Romans 2:12). In other words, we will be judged by the light we are given.

Then Paul goes on somewhat of a tangent to discuss the deeper purpose of the law and how even the Gentiles have been given some light. "For not the hearers of the law are just in the sight of God, but the doers of the law will be justified; for when Gentiles, who do not have the law, by nature do the things in the law, these, although not having the law, are a law to themselves, who show the work of the law written in their hearts, their conscience also bearing witness" (vv. 13–15). So even if the small impulse to do good is planted in the heart of every person, and such a person responds to this divine light, they are keeping the law because "love is the fulfillment of the law" (13:10).

In the same way that every person has physical life because of the power of Christ, so also does each person have spiritual light, a perception of what is right. That divine light might not be very bright and that desire to do good can be snuffed out by evil choices, yet it has been given in some measure to every person.

Earlier Paul explains that "since the creation of the world [God's] invisible attributes are clearly seen, being understood by the things that are made, even His eternal power and Godhead, so that they are with- out excuse" (Romans 1:20). Each person is given some capability to see and understand God through nature and through the mind. Though limited, it is sufficient to provide a stepping-stone toward the Creator.

BURIED WITH CHRIST

What is the meaning of baptism?

"We were buried with Him through baptism into death, that just as Christ was raised from the dead by the glory of the Father, even so we also should walk in newness of life" (Romans 6:4).

The word "baptism" comes from the Greek word "baptizo," which means to immerse, submerge, or to cleanse by dipping something under water. In one sense, it represents death—the breath "stops" while the person is under water. When we come up from the water, we are "raised with Christ" (Colossians 3:1)—resurrected to a new life.

It also represents a new birth. When a baby is born, it comes out of an envelope of water, and it takes a breath. So baptism also represents being born again. Jesus said, "Most assuredly,... unless one is born again, he cannot see the kingdom of God" (John 3:3). Baptism signifies that new start in our lives, with God in control.

Even Jesus, though He never sinned, set an example for us when He went to be baptized by John the Baptist in the Jordan River. Scripture tells us, "When He had been baptized, Jesus came up immediately from the water; and behold, the heavens were opened to Him, and He saw the Spirit of God descending like a dove and alighting upon Him" (Matthew 3:16).

Baptism is a ceremony where a person is saying, "I've turned away from my sins and have committed my life to Jesus." It is usually done publicly; a pastor immerses someone and they come up out of the water with all their old sins washed away. Baptism shows that they've accepted salvation through Christ.

Naturally, after baptism, a person's focus should be different. The Bible says, "If then you were raised with Christ, seek those things which are above, where Christ is, sitting at the right hand of God" (Colossians 3:1). If we have committed our lives to God, our center of attention should be on spiritual things. Our main focus should be on pleasing God rather than on pleasing ourselves.

THE GARDEN OF EDEN

Where was the garden of Eden located?

"The LORD God planted a garden eastward in Eden, and there He put the man whom He had formed" (Genesis 2:8).

I believe that before the flood came on the earth, everyone knew where this garden was located—as an angel was sent to guard the gates to Adam's and Eve's first home. Scripture mentions a river that came out of Eden: "Now a river went out of Eden to water the garden, and from there it parted and became four riverheads" (Genesis 2:10). The four rivers mentioned are Pishon, Gihon, Hiddekel (Tigris), and Euphrates. Keeping in mind that the world's geography was greatly altered by the flood, this area corresponds today with the country of Iraq.

I like to believe the Lord raptured this garden from this world to preserve it from the flood. If God can bring the New Jerusalem down from heaven after the millennium, He could have taken the garden up to heaven to save it (Revelation 21:2). A little anecdotal evidence for this can be found in Revelation 22:2, which speaks of the tree of life in the New Jerusalem. Since this tree was once in the garden, God might have saved the entire area and will restore it in the earth made new.

As mentioned, after the flood, the earth was radically changed. Perhaps the patriarchs had an approximate idea of where these rivers were now located by astronomy. Or it could be that the two rivers that Noah came upon after the flood reminded him of two rivers he knew before the world changed. Two of the rivers are actually missing, so you are not going to go wandering around and suddenly stumble on the garden.

Did you know that to make lots of oil and coal, it takes a tremendous amount of vegetation to be covered deep underground? Geologists today recognize that though the Middle East, rich with oil, seems largely dry and barren today, it was not always that way.

Finally, in Revelation 22:1, John sees "a pure river of water of life, clear as crystal, proceeding from the throne of God" (Revelation 22:1). That's a river I'd like to stand next to someday!

GOD'S FOREKNOWLEDGE

Why did God create our world if He knew we would fall into sin?

"Great is our Lord, and mighty in power; His understanding is infinite" (Psalm 147:5).

t is true that God is all knowing. "Do you know how the clouds are balanced, those wondrous works of Him who is perfect in knowledge?" (Job 37:16).

A lady once asked me if the Lord created our planet as some sort of cosmic experiment. In return, I asked her if she was a parent, and she said yes. I then asked, "Do parents who choose to have children not know that their kids will have free wills and make some bad choices? Of course! Yet love takes risks. God has demonstrated that all of us were made free. He even made creatures that He knew would potentially rebel."

What would it be like if the Lord only made people who were "programmed" to love Him? Obviously, there is something wrong with that because real love cannot be forced. It must be freely given. It was so important to God that humans be free moral agents who could make their own choices that He created people who could truly turn from Him.

Some people suggest that God's knowledge about what will take place in the future somehow interferes with history and people's choices. Others believe the Lord "turns off" this ability to know things ahead of time. But just as a video camera can record events without interfering with those happenings, so God's foreknowledge never violates human freedom.

When our world has run its course and Jesus comes to destroy sin forever, the entire universe will acknowledge, "Great and marvelous are Your works, Lord God Almighty! Just and true are Your ways, O King of the saints!" (Revelation 15:3). All will agree that the plans of God to create the world and permit sin to enter was handled with complete fairness and love.

The most incredible part of God's love is that He was even willing to come and die to save people who rebelled against Him. That shows me that the Lord can be trusted.

JESUS' CHILDHOOD

What did Jesus do before His ministry began?

"He went down with them and came to Nazareth, and was subject to them. ... And Jesus increased in wisdom and stature, and in favor with God and men" (Luke 2:51, 52).

When Jesus was 12 years old, He went to Jerusalem with His parents to celebrate the Passover. On his family's return trip, they soon realized He was left in Jerusalem and rushed back to search for Him. They found Jesus in the temple speaking with rabbis and religious leaders.

Jesus said to His parents, "'Why did you seek Me? Did you not know that I must be about My Father's business?'" (Luke 2:49). Some believe that at this point, Jesus separated from His parents and went to study under scholars and mystics from the Orient. They point to John 7:15, which says, "The Jews marveled, saying, 'How does this Man know letters, having never studied?'" Critics still struggle to believe that an uneducated carpenter could teach such sublime truths.

But notice the next few verses—Jesus returned to Nazareth and continued to live under the authority of His earthly parents. During His early years, Christ grew physically, mentally, and spiritually. He followed the normal growth of any other child into adulthood; except, of course, we believe that Jesus never sinned.

The Bible speaks little else of Christ's younger life. We can safely assume that Jesus worked with Joseph in the family business until the father passed away. When He came to teach in His hometown, everyone knew Him. He hadn't lived in China or Rome and become a stranger (Mark 6:3).

Jesus likely worked in the family business until John the Baptist began preaching. At that time, He knew His ministry was about to begin.

I believe Jesus was educated at the feet of His mother. Jewish children were among the most literate, and there is little reason to think that Christ grew up in a home without education. His primary lesson books were the Hebrew Scriptures and nature. It shows that a simple, quiet home where everyone helps out can enhance the growth of a child in a way no "sophisticated" curriculum ever could.

RESURRECTION ACCOUNTS

Do the Gospels differ on the events of the resurrection?

"On the first day of the week Mary Magdalene went to the tomb early, while it was still dark, and saw that the stone had been taken away from the tomb" (John 20:1).

The varying details in the resurrection accounts are complementary, not contradictory. Each writer actually focuses on a different aspect of the event. For instance, John writes about his experience with Peter. Mark looks at Mary, and Matthew seems to focus more on the women who came to the tomb. Of course, all these individuals came to the tomb but at different times.

In my study, I believe that the first one to the tomb was Mary Magdalene. After she discovered Jesus wasn't there, she ran to tell the other women. Then together they returned to the tomb, at which time an angel appeared to them.

They then left to tell others. Mary went to tell Peter and John, who immediately came to the tomb. This is when John "outran" Peter and Mary. Peter went in first, and then John went in. They saw the garments, then they left to go tell their fellow disciples. Mary eventually caught up with them and, after the two men left, she remained behind. This is when Christ appeared to her.

What about the number of angels? Depending on their vantage point, the first visitors might have seen only one angel. But when they entered the tomb, apparently another angel spoke to them. While we don't have all the details outlined, it's reasonable to believe there were two different angels.

Ultimately, these apparent differences confirm the truthfulness of the event, rather than refute it. If all four Gospels gave exactly the same story and details, we would be suspicious it was all copied and contrived. The different perspectives tell us these were the sincere observations of those who experienced that remarkable day. A careful reading of all the accounts reveals a flow of events that confirmed that Christ indeed rose from the dead!

RESOLVING MARRIAGE CONFLICTS

How do you put God first when you and your spouse disagree?

"Let nothing be done through selfish ambition or conceit, but in lowliness of mind let each esteem others better than himself" (Philippians 2:3).

God wants married couples to get along with each other. His Word says we should live harmoniously with one another (Romans 12:16) and that we should "submit to one another" in reverence to Christ (Ephesians 5:21). With ordinary conflicts, we should try as much as possible to put the other person above ourselves.

However, there are times when conflicts arise in which conscience is involved. For example, sometimes spouses disagree over religion. Sometimes God leads a person in a new direction spiritually, but the spouse doesn't see things the same way. This can lead to major conflict.

The Bible is clear that the husband should be the spiritual leader of the family (Ephesians 5:23). But if the husband asks the wife to do something that violates her conscience or violates the Word of God, she simply shouldn't do it. In a case like that, a person needs to put God above everyone else and follow where He leads (see Matthew 10:36, 37).

At the same time, we need to be sure that we aren't letting a "convenient" interpretation of Scripture get in the way of fully devoting ourselves to our spouse!

It's a tough position to be in. It can be very distressing to have your spouse opposing what your conscience tells you to do. Under those circumstances, it's best to say, "I love you and I respect you, and I hope we can work this out, but I have to put God first."

Your spouse should respect your moral convictions, but sometimes that's not the case. It requires faith and courage to stand up for what is right, but the principles of obedience to God need to have priority in your life. Try to be tactful and loving, but firm. If the Lord is leading you in another direction, you need to do what you know God wants you to do.

FORGIVENESS

Should you ever stop forgiving someone who repeatedly offends you?

"Whenever you stand praying, if you have anything against anyone, forgive him, that your Father in heaven may also forgive you your trespasses" (Mark 11:25).

A forgiving nature is one of the attributes of God. "For You, Lord, are good, and ready to forgive, and abundant in mercy" (Psalm 86:5). God wants to forgive and cleanse us from sin (1 John 1:9). His followers also need to be forgiving.

The disciple Peter asked Jesus, "Lord, how often shall my brother sin against me, and I forgive him? Up to seven times?" Peter must have thought that would be generous, but Jesus answered, "I do not say to you, up to seven times, but up to seventy times seven" (Matthew 18:21).

He then told Peter the parable about the man whose master forgave him a great debt. But instead of extending that forgiveness to others, the man had a debtor who owed him a pittance thrown into prison. "Then his master ... said to him, 'You wicked servant! I forgave you all that debt because you begged me. Should you not also have had compassion on your fellow servant, just as I had pity on you?'" (Matthew 18:32, 33). Forgiveness is not a suggestion; it is a requirement.

Jesus taught about forgiveness on several occasions. After His model prayer, which mentions forgiving our debtors, He added, "For if you forgive men their trespasses, your heavenly Father will also forgive you. But if you do not forgive men their trespasses, neither will your Father forgive your trespasses" (Matthew 6:14,15). That's pretty plain, isn't it?

This, however, does not mean you need to endlessly submit yourself to abusive behavior. It is possible to forgive a person and still accept that you cannot associate with him or her.

Likewise, there might be times when people won't acknowledge or accept your forgiveness or be willing to forgive you. We should always try to reconcile. But if you've reached out to someone, done all you could, told them you're sorry, and they still haven't accepted that, at some point you need to move on. It's not your burden to continue to grovel; the door is open for them.

SPOUSES AND SALVATION

Can a person be saved through his or her spouse?

"Do not be unequally yoked together with unbelievers. For what fellowship has righteousness with lawlessness? And what communion has light with darkness?" (2 Corinthians 6:14).

Many have asked me if it's okay, based on 1 Corinthians 7, to marry an unbeliever. Some think that such a union can result in the salvation of a spouse, almost like an automatic ticket to heaven. I don't believe that is what the apostle Paul intends to convey. While it is true that a person can have a sanctifying influence on their spouse, salvation is an individual matter.

Let's look at the passage. First, Paul writes to encourage those who are already married to an unbeliever to stay married and not get divorced: "To the married I command, yet not I but the Lord: A wife is not to depart from her husband. But even if she does depart, let her remain unmarried or be reconciled to her husband" (1 Corinthians 7:10, 11).

Then Paul goes on to explain, "A woman who has a husband who does not believe, if he is willing to live with her, let her not divorce him. For the unbelieving husband is sanctified by the wife, and the unbelieving wife is sanctified by the husband" (vv. 13, 14).

What does it mean that the "unbelieving husband is sanctified by the wife?" We find the answer in verse 16. "For how do you know, O wife, whether you will save your husband? Or how do you know, O husband, whether you will save your wife?" We also read that husbands "may be won by the conduct of their wives, when they observe your chaste conduct accompanied by fear" (1 Peter 3:1, 2). In other words, your example can be a saving influence to an unbelieving spouse. But there is no guarantee of salvation.

Again, the passage in Corinthians is specifically for couples who are already married and one becomes a Christian. If you're already married to an unbeliever, don't automatically get a divorce. Be a positive influence in his or her life. For those who are not yet married, Paul's advice is best: Do not join your life with an unbeliever.

JESUS' POWER

Did Jesus use His divine power to only do good things for others?

"These signs will follow those who believe: In My name they will cast out demons; they will speak with new tongues" (Mark 16:17).

Absolutely. When you carefully study all of the stories about Jesus written in the Gospels, His life was one of continuous service to others. Everything Christ did was to glorify God and help others. You see this in His teaching and acts of healing.

However, it is important to keep the following in mind: The power that Christ used in His work is also available to us—His people. Jesus said, "He who believes in Me, the works that I do he will do also; and greater works than these he will do, because I go to My Father" (John 14:12). Just as Christ raised the dead, so also His apostles raised the dead. Jesus taught and healed. The book of Acts records that His disciples did the same. And so may we.

Christ never used His supernatural power for any selfish reasons. He could have used His power to save Himself. He could have refreshed Himself from sleepiness while in the boat, but He chose to remain tired. He could have used His power while He was thirsting on the cross, but He had a greater mission than Himself.

Satan tempted Jesus in the wilderness to use His divine power to satisfy His agonizing hunger. The devil knew that Jesus had the power to work that miracle. He tried to provoke Christ to draw on His divinity for relief. Why would that have been such a triumph for Satan? He could have used that to sustain his charges that God required an obedience that no human could produce. If Jesus had failed to overcome the tempter with the same nature we have, and by the same means available to us, the devil would have proven that obedience is an impossible requirement. Satan understood that Jesus could not use His divine power to save Himself and to save man at the same time. This is what made the test such a severe and agonizing experience for Christ.

TWO TABLES

Why were the Ten Commandments put on two tablets instead of just one?

"Moses turned and went down from the mountain, and the two tablets of the Testimony were in his hand. The tablets were written on both sides; on the one side and on the other they were written. Now the tablets were the work of God" (Exodus 32:15, 16).

Some wonder how the commandments were divided between the two tables of stone. Some believe that there were five commandments on one table and five on the other. Others think they were split between four and six.

When you study the Ten Commandments, you see that the first four commands speak of mankind's relationship with God and the last six deal with our relationships with one another. Likewise, in the "Lord's Prayer," Matthew 6:9–15 and Luke 11:2–4, you find the first three petitions dealing with God and the last four addressing mankind's needs.

The rabbis typically divided the commandments between four and six. In fact, when Jesus was asked which was the greatest commandment, He commented on this division. " 'You shall love the LORD your God with all your heart, with all your soul, and with all your mind.' This is the first and great commandment. And the second is like it: 'You shall love your neighbor as yourself' " (Matthew 22:37–39). Then He said, "On these two commandments hang all the Law and the Prophets" (v. 40).

Some suggest that the reason the two tables were written on both sides of the stone was that one set was a copy. This idea comes from the covenant laws of the time in which both parties had a copy of the agreement.

Whatever your view, the important message is that the Ten Commandments are summarized in love for God and our fellowman, and the Lord would like to write His law on your heart. "This is the covenant that I will make with the house of Israel after those days, says the LORD: I will put My law in their minds, and write it on their hearts; and I will be their God, and they shall be My people" (Jeremiah 31:33).

God's Heart

Are there two different accounts of creation in Genesis?

"I am the LORD God of Abraham your father and the God of Isaac; the land on which you lie I will give to you and your descendants" (Genesis 28:13).

Most liberal scholars question the authenticity of the Bible, and one fervent point of their attack has been on the Pentateuch, the first five books of the Bible. Through their method of "higher criticism," they claim Moses did not write these books; rather, they say that there were at least four writers, over a long period of time, and an "editor" who pieced them together.

Genesis chapters 1 and 2 are viewed as written by two people supposedly because of different styles of writing and some alleged contradictions. For instance, the name for God, Elohim, is used in Genesis 1, and the name Jehovah is used in Genesis 2. The assumption is that this indicates different writers. But a single author can write with a different emphasis, even within the same piece of literature!

In fact, the name Elohim perfectly fits the context of Genesis 1, where this name emphasizes God's strength. The name Jehovah brings out the moral and spiritual nature of the Lord, especially in His desire to have a relationship with His people. It's interesting that both these terms are used in a single verse in Genesis 28:13.

Regarding two different creation accounts, one scholar writes, "Genesis 1 mentions the creation of man as the last of a series, and without any details, whereas in Genesis 2 man is the center of interest and more specific details are given about him and his setting. There is no incompatible duplication here at all. Failure to recognize the complementary nature of the subject-distinction between a skeleton outline of all creation on the one hand, and the concentration in detail on man and his immediate environment on the other, borders on [dogmatic]."

For me, the bottom line is that I accept by faith that Moses, under the inspiration of God, gave us an accurate account of creation in Genesis 1 and 2. The first chapter simply shows us the overall account, and the second highlights the personal connection God has with human beings.

THE NEW EARTH

Will our planet be the "new earth" after Jesus' second coming?

"Now I saw a new heaven and a new earth, for the first heaven and the first earth had passed away" (Revelation 21:1).

God created Eden and the rest of our world with perfection and beauty, but then sin came and polluted the earth. The Lord's plan was corrupted, perverted, and tainted by the devil. However, Satan will not ultimately confound God's plan. The Lord is going to create a new heaven (a new atmosphere) and a new earth.

The Bible teaches that someday "the meek... shall inherit the earth" (Matthew 5:5). It's pretty clear that, right now, proud and controlling people mostly rule the earth. But someday, this will change. Daniel says, "The kingdom and dominion, and the greatness of the kingdoms under the whole heaven, shall be given to the people, the saints of the Most High" (Daniel 7:27). The earth will not be in the same condition that it is now, for the Lord will make "a new heaven and a new earth" (Revelation 21:1).

The apostle Peter encourages us, "We, according to His promise, look for new heavens and a new earth in which righteousness dwells" (2 Peter 3:13). When will this take place? First, the righteous will be caught up to meet the Lord in the air at the second coming of Christ (1 Thessalonians 4:17). Then they will spend a millennium in heaven, living and reigning with Jesus (Revelation 20:4).

At the end of the millennium in heaven, John writes, "I saw the holy city, new Jerusalem, coming down from God out of heaven" (Revelation 21:2). The New Jerusalem is the city of God, and its new home will be this planet. There will be no pollution; it will be this Earth *made new.* In this new home, "They shall build houses and inhabit them, they shall plant vineyards and eat their fruit" and "the wolf and the lamb shall feed together" (Isaiah 65:21, 25). Our new home will be a real place!

SERVING GOD AS A SINGLE

What if you have a desire to get married but God's providence calls on you to be single?

"There are eunuchs who have made themselves eunuchs for the kingdom of heaven's sake. He who is able to accept it, let him accept it" (Matthew 19:12).

I believe some are called to serve God as single men and women. Jesus acknowledged this when He said that some are born eunuchs (referring not only to men, but to singles), some are made eunuchs, and some choose to be eunuchs. God says there are people who serve Him best in their singleness, foremost among them being Jesus.

There are other examples in the Bible. Daniel and his friends, for instance, were made eunuchs after being carried off to Babylon. They served God powerfully, even influencing nations, despite the fact they could never marry.

The apostle Paul was single, choosing that life so he could serve God more effectively. His advice to others was, "I say to the unmarried and to the widows: It is good for them if they remain even as I am; but if they cannot exercise self-control, let them marry. For it is better to marry than to burn with passion" (1 Corinthians 7:8, 9).

If you are in the place where you're wondering if the single life is what God has in mind for you or whether you should get married, don't worry about it. If God wants you to be with someone, He's going to work it out. "In all your ways acknowledge Him, and He shall direct your paths" (Proverbs 3:6).

Instead, pray, "Lord, I'm yours. I'm willing to wait for the right person—or no person." While you wait, have peace and do whatever God gives you to do, whether it's work, education, or serving Him in your local church. Do that with all your heart, and see if He doesn't surprise you with something.

Desires are normal; it's natural for every healthy male and female to feel a longing for the companionship of the opposite sex. That doesn't necessarily mean you should follow that desire. Our desires should be controlled and directed. Patiently trust in the Lord.

SUICIDE

What does the Bible say about suicide?

"Neither death nor life, nor angels nor principalities nor powers, nor things present nor things to come, nor height nor depth, nor any other created thing, shall be able to separate us from the love of God" (Romans 8:38, 39).

This is a very sensitive and difficult issue. Most of us know someone—perhaps a friend or family member—who has taken his or her own life. Some wonder whether suicide is the unpardonable sin. I don't believe so. The Bible gives no indication that suicide equals the automatic loss of salvation. It is, however, a very troubling and tragic decision that complicates an individual's destiny.

The Bible says, "The just shall live by faith" (Romans 1:17), and suicide, typically, is the result of a total loss of hope and faith. Further, the Bible commands, "You shall not murder," which naturally includes oneself. So, generally speaking, it would appear to many that if the last acts of a person's life were to lose faith and then commit "self-murder," it would not bode well for one's future fate. Instead, it's best for us to remember that where there is life, there is hope (Ecclesiastes 9:4).

But even with suicide, there can be hope because God looks at the heart. Only God truly knows the human heart, which is why He has commanded us not to judge someone's eternal destiny based upon what might be a reckless final decision.

However, I can say with total assurance that it would not be God's will for anyone to take his or her own life as an escape from this world. He loves each of us with a deeper love than we can know, and He wants to give us an abundance of life. When things get tough and emotions low, remember nothing can separate you from the love of God and that love "bears all things, believes all things, hopes all things, endures all things" (Romans 8:39; 1 Corinthians 13:7).

Some people have wondered, "Can people who commit suicide go to heaven?" It goes without saying that most suicides are the result of extreme discouragement, pain, depression, stress, unbalanced brain chemistry, and compromised thinking processes. God holds us accountable only for what we know we are doing; contemplate this:

"To him who knows to do good and does not do it, to him it is sin" (James 4:17).

God is far more merciful than we can ever imagine (see Ephesians 2:4). There are some who have taken their lives because they felt their grief or pain was more than they could bear at that particular moment in time—and in a rash decision, they ended it when maybe, had they waited but five minutes, the urge would have passed. They loved the Lord, they served the Lord, but they were in so much agony because of physical suffering or some emotional devastation or chemical change, they tragically took their own lives. We can't possibly know what all the circumstances are. We don't know what kinds of pressures and attacks they were under.

But God knows. I don't think He judges a whole life by a moment when a person might have been overwhelmed. God takes everything into account. I believe He will take every case into consideration and evaluate it individually.

If you've lost someone to suicide, place that situation in God's hands and "trust in the LORD with all your heart" (Proverbs 3:5). Remember, the Lord loves that person and wants him or her saved even more than you do. Pray, "Lord, since I don't know the answer now, I'm going to trust You. I'm going to have faith that You will do the right thing, and whatever You do I will trust." And leave it at that, because worrying about it will only tear your heart up.

EVERY TEAR

In heaven, will we have memories of everything about our life on this earth?

"God will wipe away every tear from their eyes; there shall be no more death, nor sorrow, nor crying. There shall be no more pain, for the former things have passed away" (Revelation 21:4).

If there will be no crying in heaven, some wonder if our memories will be erased of all the sad events and the people who did not make it to heaven.

It's hard to imagine, but even now there are times when there is sadness in heaven. Just as the angels rejoice when a sinner is saved, they grieve when a person is lost (Luke 15:7). Surely there was great sadness in heaven when Jesus suffered on the cross. In the same way, during the 1,000 years in heaven, we'll experience sorrow for loved ones who are not there with us. And, of course, after the millennium, as we behold the final destruction of the lost, we will share in God's sadness.

But this will also mark the end of all sorrow. It is at this point when God recreates our planet and promises to "wipe away every tear from their eyes." Just as time can heal all things, so the Lord will wipe away all tears as the ceaseless ages begin. "For behold, I create new heavens and a new earth; and the former shall not be remembered or come to mind" (Isaiah 65:17). He will give us a gift of joy that will eclipse all the former painful memories.

It's not that we couldn't recall painful memories if we wanted, as if God erased our brains. We will certainly never forget how Jesus redeemed us from sin on Calvary's cross. But after a million years in paradise, we just won't need to review our sad memories.

When speaking to His disciples about leaving, Jesus said, "A woman, when she is in labor, has sorrow because her hour has come; but as soon as she has given birth to the child, she no longer remembers the anguish, for joy that a human being has been born into the world" (John 16:21). In the same way, the glories of paradise and Jesus will overshadow all the former gloom.

BAPTISM AND SALVATION

Why do the genealogies of Christ differ between Matthew and Luke?

"Jesus ... began His ministry at about thirty years of age, being (as was supposed) the son of Joseph, the son of Heli" (Luke 3:23).

The writers of Matthew and Luke were communicating to two different groups of readers, so they approach Jesus' genealogy from different angles.

Matthew writes to a Jewish audience and establishes Jesus as the Messiah via His lineage through the promised seed of Abraham and King David, perhaps the two most prominent ancestors in Israel's history. Matthew provides this evidence to help convince people that Christ is the Anointed One from God, prophesied in Scripture. He follows the line of Joseph, Jesus' earthly father.

Luke, a physician, writes mostly to the Gentiles and follows Jesus' lineage all the way back to Adam, who was a "son of God." In other words, Christ is connected not just to the Jewish people, but to the entire human race. Because Mary's conception was through the Holy Spirit, there was some question whether God placed any essence of Joseph's DNA into Jesus. Both Matthew and Luke are careful not to firmly link Jesus as the actual son of Joseph; Luke uses the phrase "as was supposed." It is believed that Luke's lineage follows Mary's father or Joseph's father-in-law.

Ancient genealogists did not trace nor categorize lineages in the same way we do. Often, a grandfather would still be referred to as a father to a grandson. A son could be any male descendent. Not every generation was always listed. Matthew's cluster of "fourteen" generations is used to help establish Jesus with David. In Hebrew, the numerical value of David's name is 14.

Finally, let's remember that the apostle Paul warns us about getting too caught up in studying genealogies, saying not to "give heed to fables and endless genealogies, which cause disputes rather than godly edification" (1 Timothy 1:4). I'm glad that my salvation is based on my spiritual adoption. Paul writes, "Therefore know that only those who are of faith are sons of Abraham" (Galatians 3:7).

DEGREES OF REWARD

Will non-Christians who live a good life receive less punishment or possibly be saved?

"That servant who knew his master's will, and did not prepare himself or do according to his will, shall be beaten with many stripes. But he who did not know, yet committed things deserving of stripes, shall be beaten with few" (Luke 12:47, 48).

The Bible is clear that everyone is rewarded according to what they've done: "I am coming quickly, and My reward is with Me, to give to every one according to his work" (Revelation 22:12).

Jesus also seems to suggest that there will be varying degrees of punishment for the wicked. In Luke 12:48, He adds, "Everyone to whom much is given, from him much will be required; and to whom much has been committed, of him they will ask the more." So someone who knows God's will and does wrong is going to be more culpable than someone who is sinful but didn't know as much.

If everybody burns in hellfire forever, then everyone gets the same punishment. But that's not what the Bible teaches. According to Jesus, people receive different consequences. Some poor souls raised in total ignorance of right and wrong might simply be as though they were never born. Some may be burnt up quickly. People are going to suffer on judgment day, but the Bible tells us a time is coming when there is no more suffering, when all the former things are passed away (see Revelation 21:4, 5).

Scripture plainly tells us that we need Jesus in order to be saved. "Nor is there salvation in any other, for there is no other name under heaven given among men by which we must be saved" (Acts 4:12). No one else can save us.

Living a "good" life won't save us either. "No one is good but One, that is, God" (Matthew 19:17). However, there are people who never had the chance to hear about Christ or the Bible. If they followed the light God gave them through His Spirit and turned away from wrong, I imagine God could choose to save them. "Many will come from east and west, and sit down with Abraham, Isaac, and Jacob in the kingdom of heaven" (Matthew 8:11).

War in Heaven

Did the "war in heaven" take place before
or after the time of Adam and Eve?

"War broke out in heaven: Michael and his angels fought with the dragon; and the dragon and his angels fought, but they did not prevail, nor was a place found for them in heaven any longer. So the great dragon was cast out, that serpent of old, called the Devil and Satan... and his angels were cast out with him" (Revelation 12:7–9).

I believe that the Bible teaches this war began *before* our world was created. It doesn't tell us exactly how long this went on. We do know from Scripture that the devil was once an undefiled angel named Lucifer. He rebelled against God and became the fallen angel now known as Satan, meaning "adversary." In other words, the Lord did not *make* a devil.

But when did God cast Satan out of heaven? Did this war between good and evil start before or after Adam and Eve? The Bible tells us, "He who sins is of the devil, for the devil has sinned from the beginning" (1 John 3:8).

Now God created the garden of Eden and, in the context of freewill, placed a test of Adam's and Eve's loyalty. He warned them about the tree of the knowledge of good and evil. So, obviously, somebody was going to be tempting them to turn away from the Lord right from the beginning. It certainly was not God tempting them. "Let no one say when he is tempted, 'I am tempted by God'; for God cannot be tempted by evil, nor does He Himself tempt anyone" (James 1:13).

So in order for Satan to tempt Adam and Eve, he must have rebelled before the creation of our world. It might have even added to the devil's jealous rebellion when God created our first parents, because angels cannot procreate. The devil does not have creative power, but Adam and Eve could create in their own image through the union of love. Because God made man in His own image and the devil hates God, it might have inspired Satan to especially focus his anger on the first couple.

WHEN GOD SEEMS SILENT

Why does God sometimes seem silent when we need Him most?

"Behold, a woman of Canaan came out of the same coasts, and cried unto him, saying, Have mercy on me, O Lord, thou son of David; my daughter is grievously vexed with a devil. But he answered her not a word" (Matthew 15:22, 23, KJV).

Most sincere Christians have asked this important and perplexing question at some time in their lives. I think we need to remember that when we ask God for something and it seems as though He is silent, He might still be answering us, though maybe not in the way we want or expect Him to answer.

If we ask God for direction, or to relieve some stressful situation, it might seem as though nothing is happening when, in fact, He could be asking us to keep trusting and to wait patiently.

God has three answers He can give to our prayers—yes, no, or wait. If an answer doesn't come quickly, perhaps circumstances have not ripened to where God is prepared to act. Maybe other individuals are involved in our request and God is working on their hearts. The timing might not be just right. In this situation, keep praying, keep asking, keep believing, and keep trusting. If we are praying according to His will, God has promised to answer, but He will give us the answer we need at the right time. (See His promise in Psalm 32:8.)

Sometimes God has already given the answer in His Word. "Your word is a lamp to my feet and a light to my path" (Psalm 119:105). Search the Scriptures, and you might discover some light for your specific situation.

Finally, when the Canaanite woman came to Jesus and begged Him to heal her demon-possessed daughter, at first He did not answer because He was testing her faith. With determination, she continued to plead for His help. Jesus then responded, "Great is your faith! Let it be to you as you desire" (Matthew 15:28). And He healed her daughter. In this story, we see the critical importance of perseverance and faith in our prayers.

THE GREAT I AM

Who is the "I AM" spoken of in the Bible?

"Jesus said to them, 'Most assuredly, I say to you, before Abraham was, I AM'" (John 8:58).

The Scriptures teach clearly that the great "I AM" is Jesus. Remember when Moses didn't know how to identify to the Israelites which god had sent him? "God said to Moses, 'I AM WHO I AM.' And He said, 'Thus you shall say to the children of Israel, "I AM has sent me to you"'" (Exodus 3:14).

The phrase "I AM" means that God is the eternal, self-existent One. In conversations with others, we often like to know how old a person is and where they are from. With the Lord, He has always been and is everywhere. He has no beginning and no end. In the book of Revelation, He is spoken of as the "Alpha and the Omega" (Revelation 1:8, 11; 21:6). As the Creator, He is "from everlasting to everlasting" (Psalm 90:2).

We can see the connection of this sacred "I AM" name in the Gospels when Christ spoke of Himself saying, "*I am* the bread" (John 6:35), "*I am* the good shepherd" (John 10:11), and "*I am* the vine" (John 15:5).

The title of "I AM" was so clearly understood by Christ's enemies that when He used it for Himself, "They took up stones to throw at Him; but Jesus hid Himself and went out of the temple, going through the midst of them, and so passed by" (John 8:59).

One other interesting reference to the name "I AM" is found at the beginning of the Ten Commandments. Notice, "God spoke all these words, saying: 'I *am* the LORD your God, who brought you out of the land of Egypt, out of the house of bondage. You shall have no other gods before Me'" (Exodus 20:1–3). Even in God's law we find Christ exemplified!

Remember how Jesus said, "If you love Me, keep My commandments" (John 14:15)? Actually, the phrase "keep My commandments" comes right out of the Ten Commandments (Exodus 20:6; Deuteronomy 5:10). There is an obvious connection between Christ, the law, and the name "I AM."

JUDGING OTHERS

Is it always wrong to judge others?

"Do you not know that the saints will judge the world? And if the world will be judged by you, are you unworthy to judge the smallest matters? Do you not know that we shall judge angels? How much more, things that pertain to this life?" (1 Corinthians 6:2, 3).

We've all heard people echo the command, "Judge not, that you be not judged. For with what judgment you judge, you will be judged; and with the measure you use, it will be measured back to you" (Matthew 7:1, 2). This is not a universal prohibition against ever using practical judgment with other people. Jesus also said, "Do not judge according to appearance, but judge with righteous judgment" (John 7:24).

God is not saying that we aren't to use judgment to distinguish between right and wrong. Neither is He suggesting we shouldn't hold each other accountable, or that we can't help guide another person. The Bible says we should "be gentle to all, able to teach, patient, in humility correcting those who are in opposition, if God perhaps will grant them repentance, so that they may know the truth" (2 Timothy 2:24, 25).

It's appropriate to condemn a wrong act, but we have no right to condemn a person. And we should always be ready to forgive the one who commits a wrong act, just as our Father in heaven is ready to forgive the offender. Being merciful doesn't in any way condone the wrong that has been done. Just as God does, we should hate the sin, but love the sinner.

When He says, "Judge not," God is telling us we're not to pass sentence on anyone. We should be careful in that regard because when we judge and denounce other people, we're going to be judged by those standards as well. Paul wrote, "Therefore you are inexcusable, O man, whoever you are who judge, for in whatever you judge another you condemn yourself; for you who judge practice the same things" (Romans 2:1). Frequently, people who criticize and condemn others are hypocrites and are themselves guilty of the same kind of sin.

You may have asked, "Why can't we judge others?" It's very easy to be a hypocrite, to sharply or unjustly criticize others when you're not living up to your own standards. Jesus warned, "How can you say to your brother, 'Let me remove the speck from your eye'; and look, a plank is in your own eye? Hypocrite! First remove the plank from your own eye, and then you will see clearly to remove the speck from your brother's eye" (Matthew 7:4, 5). He's saying it's okay to take the speck out, but make sure you don't have a log in your eye first!

The Bible commands, "He who speaks evil of a brother and judges his brother, speaks evil of the law and judges the law. ... Who are you to judge another?" (James 4:11, 12). We should not judge another person's motives because only God can read the heart. "Man looks at the outward appearance, but the LORD looks at the heart" (1 Samuel 16:7). We can try to guess someone's motives, but we're likely to be wrong.

While we don't know the heart of any person, we should be able to tell whether their actions are in accordance with Scripture. We don't know why a person is doing something, but if it's wrong, maybe in a humble, non-offensive way, we can help and encourage that person and "restore such a one in a spirit of gentleness," while at the same time "considering yourself lest you also be tempted" (Galatians 6:1).

Although Christians should not judge the motives of others now, the Bible tells us a day will come when we will judge the world and even angels. "Judge nothing before the time, until the Lord comes, who will both bring to light the hidden things of darkness and reveal the counsels of the hearts" (1 Corinthians 4:5). Sometime after Jesus returns, God will show us the motives of those who are lost— both humans and angels—so that we can know that He has treated them fairly.

BORN AGAIN

Why is it necessary to be "born again" to be saved?

"Most assuredly, ... unless one is born again, he cannot see the kingdom of God" (John 3:3).

I f everyone is already a child of God, is it really necessary to be born again?

The Bible says, "As many as received Him, to them He gave the right to become children of God, to those who believe in His name: who were born, not of blood, nor of the will of the flesh, nor of the will of man, but of God" (John 1:12, 13). This passage says that "to become" children of God, we must believe in His name. The result of accepting Christ as your Savior is being born again.

Jesus told Nicodemus that unless he was born again, he could not see the kingdom of God. Nicodemus was initially confused by this metaphor, so Christ clarified, "Most assuredly, ... unless one is born of water and the Spirit, he cannot enter the kingdom of God. That which is born of the flesh is flesh, and that which is born of the Spirit is spirit" (John 3:5, 6). The flesh refers to our natural birth, and the Spirit speaks of our spiritual rebirth. We all have been born of the flesh, but not everyone has been born of the Spirit. (See also 1 Corinthians 15:50.)

It's a fundamental belief in Christianity that we must recognize we are sinners. Seeing that we need Jesus as our Savior, we come to Him, confess our sins, and ask Him to cleanse us and create a new heart within us. God will never force us, so unless we willingly ask Jesus into our hearts, the Lord cannot fully work within us.

In the Bible, we see John the Baptist baptizing people in the waters of the Jordan. The disciples of Christ also baptized. Baptism is a symbol of a new birth—just as when a baby emerges from its protective envelope of water and takes its first breath. This sacred ceremony is the public declaration that we're on God's side and have become His children. It's important for our own spiritual growth and as a witness to others.

Missing Sheep

What should our response be toward those who leave the church?

"You shall be called the Repairer of the Breach" (Isaiah 58:12).

I imagine everyone knows at least one person who was once walking with Jesus and was enthusiastic about being a Christian, but then he or she stopped attending church.

There are many reasons people stop going. About 2.7 million former church members reported they drifted from church activity due to their lives being too busy, while others said they no longer believed in some of the teachings of the church. But, surprisingly, the vast majority indicated that they simply didn't like the pastor or had a conflict with another member. It happens all too often. Look at these sad statistics:

- Each year 3,500 churches in America close their doors permanently.

- 150,000 people leave churches for good every week.

- 32 percent of people surveyed after leaving church reported that no one from their congregations ever contacted them.

It's unfortunate that anyone has felt ignored, rejected, ostracized, or injured by another church member or group of members. The church should be a loving and safe place, a sanctuary where sinners come to find hope, healing, and spiritual nurturing. But it doesn't always work out that way. People don't always follow the Lord's command to love one another, and often the result is that someone leaves the church.

When Jesus said, "But go rather to the lost sheep of the house of Israel" (Matthew 10:6), He was speaking of these missing members who have drifted away from the church. He was letting us know that we should be especially involved in searching for them. Rather than turning our eyes away from the problem, we should "bear one another's burdens, and so fulfill the law of Christ" (Galatians 6:2).

We should search for these people with enthusiasm, like the woman searching for her lost coin (Luke 15:8). Searching is the first step in bringing them home.

In Luke chapter 15, Jesus tells a parable about a missing sheep. In the story, the shepherd searches relentlessly until he finds it. Then he lays it on his shoulders and lovingly carries it back home. The Lord wants us to follow His example and send out search parties to look for the lost sheep among us. These missing sheep are our neighbors, friends, and family who have wandered away from the flock.

Here are some specific ways you can help someone who has left the church:

First, pray for them. God promises, "If My people who are called by My name will humble themselves, and pray and seek My face, and turn from their wicked ways, then I will hear from heaven, and will forgive their sin and heal their land" (2 Chronicles 7:14). Prayer is powerful.

Invite them back! The biggest issue facing former members is how to reconnect with the church. They could be waiting for the invitation, so you can be the one to help them find a path back. In some cases, a friendly phone call or visit might be all that is needed. Remember to treat missing members the way you would want to be treated. Offer a warm, no-pressure invitation. Be loving and nonjudgmental, and leave room for the Holy Spirit to work in their hearts.

We should also "receive one another, just as Christ received us" (Romans 15:7). Be prepared to receive with open arms those who return, as the father received the prodigal son (Luke 15:20). The shepherd in Jesus' story called his friends and neighbors in for a celebration. He told them, "Rejoice with me, for I have found my sheep which was lost!"

At the end of the parable, Jesus says, "There will be more joy in heaven over one sinner who repents than over ninety-nine just persons who need no repentance" (Luke 15:7). Shouldn't we feel the same way? Imagine how a person would feel if the entire church turned out to celebrate their return!

HOT OR COLD?

What does the Bible mean when it says we should not be lukewarm, but rather hot or cold?

"I know your works, that you are neither cold nor hot. I could wish you were cold or hot. So then, because you are lukewarm, and neither cold nor hot, I will vomit you out of My mouth" *(Revelation 3:15, 16).*

Jesus' message to the Laodicean church is where we find this verse. Laodicea was a wealthy city in Asia Minor, and, unlike the nearby cities of Hierapolis (known for its hot springs) or Colossae (known for its fresh cold water), it had to pipe in water through a long aqueduct. By the time it arrived, it was lukewarm and distasteful.

Jesus described the works of Laodicea as neither hot nor cold, but lukewarm. God detests its mediocrity because the church had opportunity to recognize its condition.

"You do not know," marked Laodicea. This church felt it was rich and needed nothing. It was in a prominent banking center known for its self-sufficiency. When an earthquake destroyed the city, it refused assistance from the emperor to rebuild. To its wealthy church, Jesus said, "You do not know that you are wretched, miserable, poor, blind, and naked" (v. 17)—strong language for a proud city. Instead, Christ offers them gold refined in fire, the pure gold of faith.

Jesus also calls Laodicea, known for its textiles, "naked" and offers them the white garments of His righteousness. And though the city was known for a medical school that sold special eye ointment, the Lord says they are "blind" and need His eye salve to see.

Yet Jesus loves this church. "As many as I love, I rebuke and chasten. Therefore be zealous and repent" (v.19). The root word for zealous (zeal) means "hot."

Being hot means being fervent about our relationship with God. Being cold describes a humble condition in which we recognize our weakness. Jesus can bless either of these attitudes, but not pride and self-sufficiency. The Lord wants this church to be on fire—"Behold I stand at the door and knock. If anyone hears My voice and opens the door, I will come in" (v. 20).

BANKRUPTCY

Should a Christian ever file bankruptcy?

"Owe no one anything except to love one another" (Romans 13:8).

When people invest in a business, always doing their best, but the business fails, I don't believe it's a sin. The creditor knew the risk. Likewise, if you borrow money with the best intentions of paying it back, and due to circumstances such as unexpected catastrophic medical bills, it's not a sin to find relief.

But suppose you borrow money promising you'll pay it back, but when you have a way to repay, in whole or in part, you decide to spend it on something nonessential. In that case, you'd be stealing. God evaluates sin based on a person's heart. (See 1 Samuel 16:7.)

There are several types of bankruptcy. One kind actually buys you time to reorganize your business so you can pay your debts, holding creditors back awhile. And there's a form of bankruptcy that basically wipes out all your debt. Another type has you pay back a portion of the debt based on your assets and income at the time.

People who have lost a spouse to tragedy are often left with tremendous debt. Sometimes the only way they're ever going to see the light of day is by taking advantage of the legal means to remove those debts. In Bible times, every 50th year was a Jubilee, during which most debts were wiped out (see Leviticus 25:9–14).

A woman once came to the prophet Elijah and said, "Your servant my husband is dead. ... And the creditor is coming to take my two sons to be his slaves" (2 Kings 4:1). Elijah didn't tell her not to pay her debt; instead, he performed a miracle to make it possible for her to pay it (2 Kings 4:2–7).

As Christians, we can be the best witnesses by always honoring our debts. Sometimes the economy turns upside-down, or other drastic circumstances arise, and people need to file bankruptcy to survive. But I personally could not rest easy if I owed a debt but chose not to pay it. Yes, it can take years to pay off credit cards and dig ourselves out, but paying back just debts is a Christian responsibility.

Human or Divine

Was Jesus human or divine when He was on this earth?

"[Jesus], being in the form of God, did not consider it robbery to be equal with God, but made Himself of no reputation, taking the form of a bondservant, and coming in the likeness of men. And being found in appearance as a man, He humbled Himself and became obedient to the point of death" (Philippians 2:6–8).

Some find it difficult to harmonize the idea that Jesus was both human and divine. If Christ was human, then how could He "see" Nathaniel praying under a fig tree? (John 1:46–49). Yet the Bible is full of statements that emphasize the divinity and the humanity of Jesus. Our Savior was 100-percent human and 100-percent divine, fully God and fully a man.

While Christ was on earth, He obviously did not have all the infinite knowledge of God swirling around in His head. After Jesus was born in Bethlehem, He grew in the natural course of human beings, both physically, mentally, and spiritually (Luke 2:52). Early on in His life, we see Him beginning to grasp His divine mission (v. 49).

As we study the life of Jesus, we see both His human nature and divine nature revealed. Jesus walked with the disciples, He ate food and slept as we sleep. Yet we also see moments when His divinity flashed through, such as on the Mount of Transfiguration (Matthew 17:2). Apparently, our Lord had access to divine knowledge and power when it was needed.

Matthew tells us that Jesus was called "Immanuel," which means "God with us" (Matthew 1:23). John describes Christ by stating, "The Word became flesh and dwelt among us, and we beheld His glory, the glory as of the only begotten of the Father, full of grace and truth" (John 1:14). He later quotes Jesus saying, "O Father, glorify Me together with Yourself, with the glory which I had with You before the world was" (17:5). Jesus limited Himself in many ways in order to identify with us, yet He was without sin (Hebrews 4:15). That is why He is our Lord and Savior!

Prayer Posture

What is the proper posture for prayer?
Is it always necessary to kneel?

"When you pray, you shall not be like the hypocrites. For they love to pray standing in the synagogues and on the corners of the streets, that they may be seen by men. Assuredly, I say to you, they have their reward" (Matthew 6:5).

In my opinion, kneeling is the best posture for formal and personal prayer. Our body language says something about how we respect God. But the Scriptures are filled with examples of people praying in various positions. God hears us when we pray, whether we are swimming, driving, or lying down.

Most examples of prayer in the Bible involve kneeling, sometimes even full prostration on the ground (Ezra 9:5, 6). This indicates a spirit of deep humility before God. The Christian practice of bowing one's head in prayer might be linked to Exodus 12:27: "The people bowed their heads and worshiped." And in the story of the publican in Luke 18, Jesus says, "The publican, standing afar off, would not lift up so much as his eyes unto heaven, but smote upon his breast, saying, God be merciful to me a sinner" (Luke 18:13).

Solomon knelt when he first prayed at the dedication of the temple (1 Kings 8:54), and then he stood when he gave the benediction and blessed the people (v. 55). If your church is standing during an invocation, but is kneeling at some other time in the service, I wouldn't create a spectacle by kneeling when everyone else is standing. This would draw too much attention to you and would be very distracting to the other worshipers.

Still, God doesn't want us to be ritualistic like the Pharisees either. The attitude and posture of our heart is the most crucial element, and though ideally there should be a kneeling prayer some time during the service, simply bowing one's head can also indicate a spirit of humility. "Ezra blessed the Lord, the great God. Then all the people answered, 'Amen, Amen!' while lifting up their hands. And they bowed their heads and worshiped the Lord with their faces to the ground" (Nehemiah 8:6).

TEMPLE REBUILT

Will the temple be rebuilt in Jerusalem before Jesus returns?

"Yet I say to you that in this place there is One greater than the temple" (Matthew 12:6).

With the constant turmoil threatening stability in the Middle East, many Bible commentators are always speculating about whether the Jewish temple will be rebuilt in the years to come. Entire Christian ministries are established to assist in the building of the temple to hasten the return of Jesus. For many, such an event will signal the start of the final events of earth's history.

However, in the same way many Christians mistakenly shift the focus from spiritual Israel to the literal Jewish nation, they are also confused on the subject of the temple. Most speculation for a rebuilt temple springs from a vague reference in 2 Thessalonians 2 dealing with the antichrist: "Let no one deceive you by any means; for that Day will not come unless the falling away comes first, and the man of sin is revealed, the son of perdition, who opposes and exalts himself above all that is called God or that is worshiped, so that he sits as God in the temple of God, showing himself that he is God" (vv. 3, 4).

Many say that for the antichrist to sit in the temple, it will need to be rebuilt. Those who support this belief are known as "Christian Zionists," and they include such popular writers as Hal Lindsey, Tim LaHaye, and John Hagee. Their published book sales exceed 70 million copies—including the popular *Left Behind* series. Their beliefs are endorsed by some of the largest theological institutions.

But are they correct? To begin, let's go to 1 Chronicles 17:11, 12: "When your days are fulfilled … I will set up your seed after you, who will be of your sons; and I will establish his kingdom. He shall build Me a house, and I will establish his throne forever." This prophecy given to King David says his offspring will build the temple.

This text is one of the clearest examples of a dual prophecy found in Scripture. But what does this mean? Will the temple be rebuilt in Jerusalem before Jesus returns?

Dual prophecies have both a physical and spiritual fulfillment. Solomon, the son of David, built the physical temple. But this prophecy also applies spiritually to Jesus, the true "Son of David," who is to build a temple and kingdom that will last forever.

Jesus' prophecy that the temple would be destroyed inspired the most intense rejection of His teachings. (See Matthew 24:1, 2.) In Mark 14:58, Jesus says, "I will destroy this temple that is made with hands, and within three days I will build another made without hands." Of course, Jesus is speaking of rebuilding a temple not of stone, but of flesh. Many refused this teaching (John 2:20, 21) and even mocked Jesus for it while He was on the cross (Matthew 27:40).

Yet when Jesus died, the veil in the earthly temple ripped in two from the top to bottom (Matthew 27:51), signifying that the temple no longer held meaning. A temple for sacrifice today would be useless, and it would not be the house of God.

The New Testament consistently presents the idea that the temple is the body of Jesus. Ephesians 2:19–22 says, "You are no longer strangers and foreigners, but fellow citizens with the saints and members of the household of God, having been built on the foundation of the apostles and prophets, Jesus Christ Himself being the chief cornerstone, in whom the whole building, being fitted together, grows into a holy temple in the Lord, in whom you also are being built together for a dwelling place of God in the Spirit."

Even after God provides all this evidence that His temple is a spiritual one, many Christians are waiting for the Jews to receive a construction permit to rebuild a temple on the site where a Muslim mosque now sits. However, there is no prophecy, promise, or commandment that says the physical temple would ever be rebuilt after the Romans razed it nearly 2,000 years ago.

IN JESUS' NAME

Is it necessary to pray "In Jesus' name" at the end of every prayer?

"Whatever you ask in My name, that I will do, that the Father may be glorified in the Son" (John 14:13).

J esus actually commands us to pray in His name. He says, "Most assuredly, I say to you, whatever you ask the Father in My name He will give you" (John 16:23). This doesn't mean, however, that just saying His name has some kind of magical power.

Suppose I go to a complete stranger asking for a favor. They're not likely to listen to my request. But if I bring them a letter from their best friend, someone they love, and it's signed by their best friend—well, that could make a big difference. I say to them, "Look, I've come in the name of Henry, and here's a letter from Henry, signed by him. Can you help me with this problem?" If they love Henry, and I'm coming in Henry's name, they will listen to me.

Jesus told us, "I am the way, and the truth, and the life. No one comes to the Father except through Me" (John 14:6). When we come to the Father, we come in the name of the Lord Jesus and say, "Please, hear my prayer. Not because I deserve it. I've been alienated from you by sin. But because of your love for your Son, please honor my request for His sake." That's really what it means to pray in Jesus' name. It can also mean to pray with the mind and the spirit of Christ and with the same attitude that Jesus had.

Of course, the Father loves us too; He wants us to come to Him. That's why He sent Jesus to bridge the gap. Jesus said, "In that day you will ask in My name, and I do not say to you that I shall pray the Father for you; for the Father Himself loves you, because you have loved Me, and have believed that I came forth from God" (John 16:26, 27).

BIBLICAL DIVORCE

What does the Bible say about divorce?

"Whoever divorces his wife, except for sexual immorality, and marries another, commits adultery; and whoever marries her who is divorced commits adultery" (Matthew 19:9).

Divorce came into the world only because of sin. It was never meant to be part of the human experience. God intended that a man and woman in marriage become so closely united in purpose, being, and existence that they are literally "one flesh." And two lives so intertwined cannot be divided without causing great pain and emotional scarring.

Sadly, the plague of divorce is now so common in our society that it's doubtful there is a soul in America who hasn't been impacted by it one way or another. Perhaps you've been through it yourself... or perhaps a friend, parent, or child of yours.

The statistics are terrible enough: Between 40 and 50 percent of all first marriages end in divorce. That means almost half the people who get married will, sooner or later, divorce. What's worse is that 67 percent of second marriages will end up in divorce too. Perhaps third marriages are charmed? Not at all, as about 74 percent of those go down the tubes as well. Indeed, about 25 percent of adults in America are divorced.

Meanwhile, more than one million children each year in America experience the breakup of their parents. *One million!* Only God knows the very real heartache, the suffering, and the trauma experienced by those who are directly impacted by divorce.

When the Pharisees came to Jesus with a question about divorce, He talked about how a man and his wife become one flesh and how man should not separate what God has joined together (see Matthew 19:4–6). He further explained: "I say to you, whoever divorces his wife, except for sexual immorality, and marries another, commits adultery; and whoever marries her who is divorced commits adultery" (verse 9).

Now, if this were the only statement in the Bible regarding marriage, it would seem that, according to Jesus, there is just one biblical ground for divorcing and then remarrying. Of course, the Bible and Jesus have more to say on marriage than just this passage.

However strict the above passage appears, it simply shows how sacrosanct marriage is supposed to be and why a couple, a church community, and even nations are under a divine obligation to protect the institution of marriage.

While God hates divorce, there is a time or two in the Bible when He actually commands it. Whenever someone got married to a person whom they later discovered was still legally married to another, they were to end the marriage.

Another valid reason for divorce is abandonment by an unbelieving partner, as when a non-Christian spouse walks away from a marriage. The Bible says, "If the unbeliever departs, let him depart; a brother or a sister is not under bondage in such cases" (1 Corinthians 7:15).

If a person is married and his or her spouse violates their marriage vows, that person has "biblical grounds" for divorce; it is permissible by Bible standards. According to Scripture, the innocent party may re-marry, but the guilty party may not as long as the ex-spouse remains unmarried and chaste. To do so would be to commit adultery again. (See Luke 16:18.)

Although adultery gives the offended spouse the right to divorce, it doesn't mean he or she must do so. Many marriages damaged by unfaithfulness have been salvaged, and many couples would do them-selves and their kids a big favor to try to make the marriage work despite the pain of infidelity.

Regardless of how scrambled your nuptial history might be, Jesus promises, "All that the Father gives Me will come to Me, and the one who comes to Me I will by no means cast out" (John 6:37). We all are sinful and in need of mercy. We should be careful not to judge others who are divorced. And if we have been divorced against biblical principles, there is forgiveness for us too. God offers healing, grace, and comfort to those who have been traumatized by divorce.

ONCE SAVED, ALWAYS SAVED

Once you are saved, can you ever lose your salvation?

*"Let us hold fast the confession of our hope without wavering,
for He who promised is faithful" (Hebrews 10:23).*

There are many examples in the Bible of people who had a saving relationship with God and were filled with the Spirit, but then they turned away ... such as King Saul and Judas. Jesus will never let go of us, but we can let go of Him. We always have that freedom.

The concept that once you are saved you can never be lost is unbiblical. People sometimes turn from God after following Him for a time. Peter puts it like this: "But it has happened to them according to the true proverb: 'A dog returns to his own vomit,' and, 'a sow, having washed, to her wallowing in the mire'" (2 Peter 2:22).

On the other extreme, some people believe that you need to walk every day in doubt of your relationship with the Lord. Yet the Bible is clear that we can walk in assurance. Paul writes, "Being confident of this very thing, that He who has begun a good work in you will complete it until the day of Jesus Christ" (Philippians 1:6). Another verse says, "Looking unto Jesus, the author and finisher of our faith" (Hebrews 12:2).

According to the Bible, the notion that once a person is saved he cannot be lost is just not true. One of the clearest verses in Scripture states:

"When a righteous man turns away from his righteousness and commits iniquity, and does according to all the abominations that the wicked man does, shall he live? All the righteousness which he has done shall not be remembered; because of the unfaithfulness of which he is guilty and the sin which he has committed, because of them he shall die" (Ezekiel 18:24).

In other words, a person who was righteous can turn away from God and be lost. If a person is saved and cannot lose his salvation, why would he need to "hold fast" and not waver according to Hebrews 10:23? Because God has given people the freedom of choice.

As we consider the false aspects of "once saved, always saved," we should remember that while Jesus will never let go of us, we can let go of Him. The danger of the teaching that once you are saved you cannot be lost is that it takes away our free will. We're always free to choose to love or reject the Lord. God does not take away our freedom once we accept Him.

Notice this example in the writings of the apostle Paul:

"Do you not know that those who run in a race all run, but one receives the prize? Run in such a way that you may obtain it. And everyone who competes for the prize is temperate in all things. Now they do it to obtain a perishable crown, but we for an imperishable crown. Therefore I run thus: not with uncertainty. Thus I fight: not as one who beats the air. But I discipline my body and bring it into subjection, lest, when I have preached to others, I myself should become disqualified" (1 Corinthians 9:24–27).

Paul was saying that even as an apostle of Jesus, he could lose his salvation. That's why Jesus said, "Not everyone who says to Me, 'Lord, Lord,' shall enter the kingdom of heaven, but he who does the will of My Father in heaven" (Matthew 7:21). Notice how some respond: "Many will say to Me in that day, 'Lord, Lord, have we not prophesied in Your name, cast out demons in Your name, and done many wonders in Your name?' And then I will declare to them, 'I never knew you; depart from Me, you who practice lawlessness!'" (vv. 22, 23).

Those who come to Christ and join the church do not necessarily continue on the pathway to heaven. Some who confess Jesus and even do great works in the name of Christ will be lost. Making a profession, such as, "I am saved," does not guarantee a genuine, living relationship with Jesus.

I want to highlight that God does not want us to live in fear. John writes, "There is no fear in love; but perfect love casts out fear" (1 John 4:18).

As long as we abide in Christ, we have nothing to fear. But when we take our hand out of His hand and we choose to turn from His will and go our own way, then we lose this assurance. But as long as we are placing our lives in the hands of the Almighty, we don't have to live in fear and doubt. God doesn't want us to have that kind of experience.

I believe that it's important for us to daily rededicate our lives to the Lord. That doesn't mean that we're lost every day. Paul said, "I die daily" (1 Corinthians 15:31). What he means by that is, "I choose every day to die to self and be born again unto God." On a daily basis we rededicate ourselves to God. That doesn't mean you're lost and saved and lost and saved...as if you're on a spiritual roller coaster. Jesus taught us to pray, "Give us this day our daily bread" (Matthew 6:11). We live on the basis of daily trusting in the Lord.

Some Christians do advocate the doctrine of eternal security. The Bible teaches that God leaves the door open for us to change our minds at any time. Salvation is not based upon only one irrevocable act or choice of the past, but upon a continuous, personal relationship of the believer with Christ. When the decision to break the love relationship is made by willful disobedience, the believer ceases to be a true believer and forfeits any assurance of salvation.

THE RIGHT CHURCH

How can you know for sure which religion is the right one?

"The dragon was enraged with the woman, and he went to make war with the rest of her offspring, who keep the commandments of God and have the testimony of Jesus Christ" *(Revelation 12:17).*

There are a lot of religions out there. Assuming you believe in the Bible, you've accepted Christianity. But how do you know which church is right?—after all, there are so many denominations!

There are many good churches, and I believe there are good Christians in every church. I believe the majority of the saved are not in my denomination, but that doesn't mean I believe every church is right. I also believe there is only one truth, and that's what we should base our decision on. But again, there are Christian people who love the Lord and are following the light they have in every persuasion.

In selecting a church, there should always be an ongoing search for truth, and the Bible needs to be the foundation. In Revelation 12, you read about the bride of Christ, and the Bible lists several criteria. It identifies some of the important characteristics of God's church in the last days.

The most outstanding characteristic is found in the last verse of that chapter. That verse says that the dragon, which represents the devil, is angry with the woman. We know this woman, the bride of Christ, represents God's church; she is clothed with light. Remember that Jesus said to His followers, "You are the light of the world" (Matthew 5:14). Furthermore, in both the Old and the New Testaments a woman is a symbol of God's people.

As the Scripture continues, the dragon goes "to make war with the rest of her offspring" (verse 17). Now, here are their characteristics: These people "keep the commandments of God and have the testimony of Jesus Christ." The Bible explains that last phrase: "The testimony of Jesus is the spirit of prophecy" (Revelation 19:10). So the two outstanding characteristics of God's people in the last days are that they keep God's Ten Commandments and they have the spirit of prophecy.

ARMOR OF GOD

How am I supposed to "put on" the armor of God?

"Take up the whole armor of God, that you may be able to withstand in the evil day, and having done all, to stand" *(Ephesians 6:13).*

The primary focus of Scripture is the ongoing conflict between Christ and Satan. Revelation tells us that what began as a cosmic war in heaven will soon end in Armageddon. In this showdown between the forces of good and the powers of evil, truth and light are under constant attack from deception and darkness. And like it or not, every single one of us is involved.

The battleground for this intense spiritual struggle is the human heart. Both Jesus and the devil are supremely interested in winning possession of our minds and hearts. The Bible says, "We do not wrestle against flesh and blood, but against principalities, against powers, against the rulers of the darkness of this age, against spiritual hosts of wickedness in the heavenly places" (Ephesians 6:12). For this reason, Christians are called to be more than peaceful spectators in this conflict. We must be committed front-line commandos.

When we talk about putting on the armor of God—the helmet of salvation, the belt of truth, the sword of the Word of God, etc.— we're obviously not speaking literally. These are symbols. We don't walk around with a sword or a war helmet. Although our armor and weapons are spiritual, this does not mean they are unreal or ineffective. "Though we walk in the flesh, we do not war according to the flesh. For the weapons of our warfare are not carnal but mighty in God for pulling down strongholds" (2 Corinthians 10:3, 4).

We must put on the unfailing armor of God—all of it! This is where many Christians fall short. They take some of the armor but forget one or two parts of the suit; sometimes, they might pay an eternal price for their neglect. Under the inspiration of the Holy Spirit, the apostle Paul attaches a spiritual association to seven implements of earthly armor. Let's next consider each of these articles of defense one by one to see what we can learn.

The first item of spiritual armor mentioned in Ephesians 6 is the belt of truth. The spiritual significance is that God does not want us to simply point at the truth; He wants us to wear it and have it wrapped about us. Wearing the belt of truth also means wearing Christ, for He is "the way, the truth, and the life" (John 14:6).

Wearing the breastplate of righteousness is always in partnership with the robe of Jesus' righteousness. The only way we can experience victory in battle against the devil is through confidence that the righteousness of Jesus covers our hearts and that we are forgiven.

When the devil sends his flaming arrows of temptation, we are to hold up the shield of faith, the shield bearing the name of our King of kings, Jesus. Through faith in His name, we can resist any enticement. "No temptation has overtaken you except such as is common to man; but God is faithful, who will not allow you to be tempted beyond what you are able, but with the temptation will also make the way of escape, that you may be able to bear it" (1 Corinthians 10:13).

In the Bible, the foot is a symbol for the direction or "the walk" of a person's life. Are you walking with the Lord? Are you going in the right direction? The Scriptures explain how to have a sacred walk. But it's hard to walk when you're sliding. Having our feet "shod with the preparation of the gospel of peace" (Ephesians 6:15 KJV) gives us good footing—and prevents backsliding.

The Bible says, "How beautiful upon the mountains are the feet of him who brings good news, who proclaims peace, who brings glad tidings of good things, who proclaims salvation" (Isaiah 52:7). As we become involved in spreading the good news, it will strengthen us against the enemy's attacks.

Your body has seven openings from the neck up: two nostrils, two ears, two eyes, and one mouth. Pivotal to each person's salvation are their choices concerning what they allow to enter their minds through these senses. Jesus said, "The lamp of the body is the eye" (Luke 11:34). Also, we read, "Apply your heart to instruction, and your ears to words of knowledge" (Proverbs 23:12) and, "Put away from you a deceitful mouth, and put perverse lips far from you" (Proverbs 4:24).

We need to be careful what we watch, what we listen to, what we say, and what we eat and drink. These things affect who we are. Ask God for that helmet of salvation. Think of it as a space helmet, where you've got a heavenly atmosphere to breathe. It's protecting you from harmful influences. We need to firmly strap the helmet of salvation in place and guard these avenues to the soul.

When the Bible talks about the sword, it means you need to get to know your Bible. The other armaments in God's arsenal are defensive in nature, but the sword is primarily an offensive weapon. When Jesus fought the devil, He quoted Scripture. "Your word I have hidden in my heart, that I might not sin" (Psalm 119:11).

The last of the armaments is really an attitude. Any general knows that victory almost always depends on which army has the element of surprise. The Scripture says, "Watch and pray, lest you enter into temptation" (Matthew 26:41). We should "pray without ceasing" (1 Thessalonians 5:17). This does not mean we go about on our knees all day; rather, we must be constantly aware of God's presence and that there is an enemy stalking us.

How can we stand? How can we fight? Paul gives us the answer: "Be strong in the Lord and in the power of His might" (Ephesians 6:10). Jesus said, "Without Me you can do nothing" (John 15:5).

TRUE AND FALSE PROPHETS

How do you know if a prophet is true or false?

"To the law and to the testimony! If they do not speak according to this word, it is because there is no light in them" (Isaiah 8:20).

Jesus spoke to this question when giving us signs of the end. "Take heed that no one deceives you. For many will come in My name, saying, 'I am the Christ,' and will deceive many" (Matthew 24:4, 5). Later He warned, "False christs and false prophets will rise and show great signs and wonders to deceive" (Matthew 24:24).

Notice that Jesus did not say there would never be any more true prophets. The gift of prophecy was promised to the church and was not cut off at the time of Christ. Luke writes, "In the last days … I will pour out of My Spirit on all flesh; your sons and your daughters shall prophesy" (Acts 2:17).

There are Bible tests you can apply to identify a true prophet. Here are some examples: First, prophets don't express their private opinions on spiritual matters. "Prophecy never came by the will of man, but holy men of God spoke as they were moved by the Holy Spirit" (2 Peter 1:21). Second, a prophet never speaks in contradiction to the Word. Their teachings are in harmony with Scripture.

The Bible provides further information on different types of false prophets in Deuteronomy 18:10–12 and Revelation 21:8. It identifies charmers (someone who casts spells), observer of times (astrologers), sorcerers (someone who claims to speak with the dead), consulters of familiar spirits (mediums), users of divination (fortune tellers), witches (female psychics), and wizards (male psychics).

God has given His church the spirit of prophecy (Revelation 19:10) for the purpose of building up believers (1 Corinthians 14:22). True prophets live a godly life (Matthew 7:15–20), have predictions that come true (Deuteronomy 18:20–22), and are called to service by God (Isaiah 6:1–10). We should follow the apostle Paul's advice to "Despise not prophesyings. Prove all things; hold fast that which is good" (1 Thessalonians 5:20, 21).

Some people ask, "Do you think true prophets could appear between now and Jesus' second coming?" Based on Joel's prophecy

(Joel 2:28–32), it certainly appears possible. There also will be false prophets (Matthew 7:15; 24:11, 24). We must be prepared to test prophets by the Bible (Isaiah 8:19, 20; 2 Timothy 2:15), heeding their counsel only if they are genuine—and rejecting them if they are counterfeit.

God knows when prophets are needed to wake people up, warn them, and turn them to Jesus and His Word. He sent a prophet (Moses) to lead His people out of Egypt (Hosea 12:13). He sent a prophet (John the Baptist) to prepare people for Jesus' first coming (Mark 1:1–8). He also promised prophetic messages for these end-times. God sends prophets to point us to the Bible; to strengthen, encourage, and assure us; and to make us like Jesus so we will be "blameless" when the Master returns. Without the help of a prophet, many will be lost through backsliding, sleeping spiritually, and being too busy. So let's welcome prophetic messages and praise God for sending them for our personal good.

Many recognize that most churches today do not have the gift of prophecy. Why is that? Because God often sends prophets to His church only when it is keeping His commandments. Notice how Lamentations 2:9 puts it: "The law is no more; her prophets also find no vision from the LORD." Please also review the following texts: Ezekiel 7:26; Jeremiah 26:4–6; Ezekiel 20:12–16; and Proverbs 29:18. These statements verify that when God's people disregard His commandments, He sends no prophet. When they begin to obey His commands, He sends a prophet to assist, encourage, and guide. So when God's remnant church for the end-times emerged keeping His commandments, it was time for a prophet.

And God sent one—right on schedule.

CHRISTMAS & EASTER

Is it right for churches to display a nativity for Christmas or a cross for Easter?

"He who observes the day, observes it to the Lord and he who does not observe the day, to the Lord he does not observe it. He who eats, eats to the Lord, for he gives God thanks; and he who does not eat, to the Lord he does not eat, and gives God thanks" *(Romans 14:6).*

The apostle Paul's guidance to the church helps us recognize that there are some battles not worth entering. Many people ask me about Easter and Christmas, and I would suggest you be careful not to "major in minors."

There is no command in the Bible that we should worship religious icons like the cross. It's a good symbol for helping people recognize a church as being Christian, but there is no Scripture telling us we must wear a cross around our necks or carry them around. The Bible teaches us to bear the cross of Christ, meaning to follow in the path of self-denial.

If a church wants to portray a nativity scene, especially to help young people visualize and remember the birth of Christ, I think it can be a good thing. But keep in mind, the shepherds and wise men did not visit Jesus at the same time. We also don't know exactly when Jesus was born. My greater concern over Christmas is that most people do not think of Christ. They are much more interested in the mall and using credit cards to buy—with money they don't have—lots of things that others don't need.

One guideline we should always keep in mind with symbols is the second commandment. God said, "You shall not make for yourself a carved image—any likeness of anything that is in heaven above, or that is in the earth beneath, or that is in the water under the earth; you shall not bow down to them nor serve them" (Exodus 20:4, 5). While you might never bow down in front of a nativity scene or an Easter cross, there are many religious traditions that teach otherwise.

WALKING AFTER THE SPIRIT

How does one walk after the spirit and not the flesh?

"There is therefore now no condemnation to those who are in Christ Jesus, who do not walk according to the flesh, but according to the Spirit" (Romans 8:1).

As Christians, we have two natures at war within us—the spirit and the flesh. "The flesh lusts against the Spirit, and the Spirit against the flesh; and these are contrary to one another, so that you do not do the things that you wish" (Galatians 5:17). The carnal, or physical, desires of the flesh want to be satisfied selfishly. However, the spirit strives to be pure, do God's will, and obey His commandments. The latter is the higher nature we should aim to please. Peter and other New Testament writers speak about this war between the spirit and the flesh.

In Romans 8, Paul is encouraging Christians to walk after our spiritual natures and not our fleshly desires. He describes this difficult battle in Romans 7: "I am carnal, sold under sin. For what I am doing, I do not understand. For what I will to do, that I do not practice; but what I hate, that I do" (vv. 14, 15). There is a simple, but not always easy, solution to this dilemma.

Here is a crude but effective illustration. Imagine you have two dogs of the same breed. You feed one of your dogs the very best dog food, and you pet and groom him for attention, take him out for walks, and provide plenty of fresh water and rest. But the other dog you chain to a post, don't provide food, water, exercise, or attention at any time. Now imagine releasing the two dogs in the same area. Eventually, they'll do battle for the territory. Who will win? It's easy to guess that the dog that is well nourished and exercised will conquer the starved animal.

It's the same with the battle between our two natures. The way you win the battle is decided by which nature you feed. If you feed the spirit by reading God's Word, praying, fellowshipping, and sharing your faith, you will strengthen your spiritual nature and make more room for the Holy Spirit.

As we work toward strengthening our spiritual nature, we need to keep our focus on the things of God. "Those who live according to the flesh set their minds on the things of the flesh, but those who live according to the Spirit, the things of the Spirit" (Romans 8:5). Furthermore, there are certain pitfalls to avoid. Whenever we choose to feed our fleshly nature with worldly amusements and sensual gratification, for instance, our carnal nature will be on the throne and our spirit will lose the battle.

The devil uses worldly reading materials, music, television, and movies, often disguising them as "family entertainment," to tempt us and numb our spiritual sensors. But these instant satisfactions have potentially terrible eternal consequences. They will make your spiritual muscles limp and weak. Remember, when temptation comes, whatever side we have strengthened will win the battle. This is literally a life-and-death struggle, "for to be carnally minded is death, but to be spiritually minded is life and peace" (Romans 8:6).

The good news is that if we put our trust in Him, the Lord will make sure we succeed in this effort. He promises to strengthen us. "I can do all things through Christ who strengthens me" (Philippians 4:13). He reminds us that He is "able to do exceedingly abundantly above all that we ask or think, according to the power that works in us" (Ephesians 3:20). And He assures us that we can triumph through His power. "Thanks be to God, who gives us the victory through our Lord Jesus Christ" (1 Corinthians 15:57).

Every day, we're making a series of little decisions to walk after the flesh or after the spirit. Pray daily, even hourly, for God's protection and always be mindful when investing time and resources in worldly amusements. Real satisfaction is found in the Prince of Peace, not in empty worldly pleasures.

THOUGHTS THAT DEFILE

Can a thought be a sin?

"Let the wicked forsake his way, and the unrighteous man his thoughts; let him return to the LORD, and He will have mercy on him; and to our God, for He will abundantly pardon" *(Isaiah 55:7).*

Logically speaking, we know that all wrongdoing begins with a thought. It has always been this way. Even sin itself began with a thought (see Isaiah 14:12, 13). And the Bible tells us that mankind was so wicked before the flood that "every intent of the thoughts of his heart was only evil continually" (Genesis 6:5).

In Matthew 5:21, 22, our Lord says, "You have heard that it was said to those of old, 'You shall not murder, and whoever murders will be in danger of the judgment.' But I say to you that whoever is angry with his brother without a cause shall be in danger of the judgment." Jesus is addressing the danger of even thinking angry thoughts. Furthermore, we read in verses 27 and 28: "You have heard that it was said to those of old, 'You shall not commit adultery.' But I say to you that whoever looks at a woman to lust for her has already committed adultery with her in his heart." The Lord is saying that sin is not always an action; it's an attitude. Sin is first conceived in our thoughts.

Another time, Jesus listed evil thoughts among sins that defile (see Mark 7:21–23). In the Sermon on the Mount, He spent more time talking about the attitude of pride and sinful thoughts than the actual deeds, because virtually every sinful deed originates with a sinful thought in the mind.

However, a wrong thought is not necessarily a sin. Obviously, being tempted is not a sin. During a temptation, something wrong is being proposed. At that point, it's only a thought. But watch out! Holding on to it, dwelling on it, will cause it to gain momentum. You want to be able to dismiss that thought promptly. We can do that only with God's help. In order to resist and squelch sin, we need to begin by asking the Lord to cleanse our minds and guide our thoughts with the Holy Spirit.

Going to Church

Can a person find favor with God by living biblically but not going to church?

"The Lord added to the church daily those who were being saved" (Acts 2:47).

First, it's important to note that there will be many people in heaven who were not affiliated with a church, either because they did not have that opportunity or another reason that prevents them from the privilege. But one of the most important principles of Christianity is that we are saved into the body of Christ, which is another name for the church. When you are baptized, you become part of Christ's body.

So I would ask in return: Why would a person say he loves God and His truth, but does not wish to fellowship with His people? That's one reason God wants us in church—because it has people with similar beliefs. It helps bolster our faith and makes us accountable. It is also an excellent environment in which to increase our capacity to love one another. People learn their most important lessons of love in the context of their biological families. Church families follow the same dynamic—especially with new believers.

If a person says, "I believe in God and want to be saved and baptized, but I don't want to go to church," it sounds to me like a man saying to his bride, "I love you, I want to marry you—but I don't want to live with you." It's saying you want the benefits of marriage but not the relationship that goes with it. Part of the Christian experience is having a relationship within the fellowship of believers.

I lived as a hermit once—up in a cave and away from society. In that kind of solitude, you have a tendency to become eccentric. Isolating oneself from society begins to affect your mind; your brain sort of atrophies. You become socially inept. In the same way, it's important for Christians to be social with fellow believers in corporate worship to avoid becoming spiritually inept. It's God's gift—so I encourage each Christian to find a biblical church in which they can grow into mature members of God's family.

Church Music

Does the Bible say anything about the type of music we play or instruments we should use in church worship?

"Sing to Him a new song; play skillfully with a shout of joy" (Psalm 33:3).

This is a good and a big question because it addresses a very sensitive issue—where to draw the line in church music. First, I've worshiped with conservative brethren who don't use any instruments in church. They have beautiful voices, and they sing and harmonize without instruments. That's fine, and I believe the Lord has no problem with this. But I don't agree that it's wrong for Christians to use instruments in church.

King David played harps in his praising the Lord and wrote, "Praise the LORD with the harp; make melody to Him with an instrument of ten strings" (Psalm 33:2). There were also instruments played in the sanctuary at God's instruction (see 2 Samuel 6:5). Furthermore, just because a song is contemporary doesn't make it wrong. Biblically, it's appropriate to sing a new song of praise to God. In fact, nine times the Bible mentions singing a "new song."

I think you should consider two things when finding the right balance: the music and the lyrics. Both need to be something God can bless. Some Christian groups sing beautiful, profound lyrics—but the music sounds like a car crash. Sometimes you can't even tell what they're saying! Then you've got the other extreme: reverent music but with repetitive or unbiblical words. That's no better.

Church music should be something that elevates our appreciation for the Lord. That's the kind of music that God will sanction, especially in His house of worship. It should be worshipful and convey a sense of reverence and love. It shouldn't appeal to our lower natures with heavy syncopated rhythms that encourage dance fever. Some music can bring about baser things in us; science affirms this! I used to attend rock concerts, and I could easily see what the music did to people.

So in considering music, we need to ask: Is the music enhancing the words and lifting our souls heavenward, or is it bringing out the animalistic side of our natures? Jesus said, "By their fruits you will know them" (Matthew 7:20).

Robes of Light

Some say that when we're in heaven, we'll be wearing robes of light. Is this biblical?

"Whenever the children of Israel saw the face of Moses, that the skin of Moses' face shone, then Moses would put the veil on his face again, until he went in to speak with Him" (Exodus 34:35).

The Bible does talk about angels that appear to be clothed with light, but nowhere in the Bible will you find the words "robes of light." Let's go back to Eden to get a clear picture of what it might be like for us in heaven.

A major misconception is that Adam and Eve were streaking around the garden naked like a newborn! But in reality, Adam and Eve had garments of light that clothed them—an aura of light if you will—because they were righteous and they dwelled in the presence of God. Let me explain from the Bible why I believe this is true.

When Moses spent 40 days and 40 nights on the mountain talking to the Lord, he came down and was glowing. The Bible says he was shining so brilliantly that the people said, "Veil your face. We can't even look on you." Those who dwell in the presence of the holy God, those who are righteous, are surrounded by an aura of light.

Jesus said to the church, "You are the light of the world." I don't believe the Lord is going to have cotton, linen, wool, or camel hair robes in the kingdom. When Adam and Eve sinned, the light went out and they were suddenly aware of their nakedness. They had no artificial clothing in the garden; that's why it says they were naked. But they weren't streaking around and suddenly realized it after eating the fruit. That would make it sound like the fruit actually made them smarter.

In the kingdom, when it talks about the saints who have these robes, I believe that these are living robes of light. It's based on what the angels wear. The Bible speaks of the angels of light. I don't think they've got weaving looms in heaven.

BEFORE SINAI

How did the Israelites know how to behave
before the Ten Commandments were given?

*"The works of His hands are verity and justice; all His precepts
are sure. They stand fast forever and ever, and are done in truth
and uprightness" (Psalm 111:7, 8).*

God's law is eternal. Since sin is the transgression of the law and sin existed before Sinai, then there must have been a law before the time of Moses. In Genesis, you can actually find some of the commandments spoken about before Sinai. For example, see Genesis 35:1–4 for a reference to the first commandment. In addition, it was transmitted orally from person to person.

However, by the time of Moses, after the people had been in slavery under Egypt, and thereby under the influence of a pagan religion, their memory had been corrupted and diluted. That's why Moses wrote the first five books of the Bible, so his people would not be confused. Of course, God ultimately wrote the Ten Commandments so there would never have to be any guessing about what's right and wrong.

To show this point: Long before Moses wrote the Ten Commandments onto scrolls, God said to Cain, "If you do well, will you not be accepted? And if you do not do well, sin lies at the door" (Genesis 4:7). The Bible also records, "Abraham obeyed My voice and kept My charge, My commandments, My statutes, and My laws" (Genesis 26:5). Joseph also knew it was a sin to commit adultery with Potiphar's wife. He said, "How then can I do this great wickedness, and sin against God?" (Genesis 39:9). He evidently knew adultery was a sin before the Ten Commandments were written. It had been passed on to him, so he knew God's law.

Originally, God's law went from Adam orally, straight out of the garden of Eden, to become part of the oral tradition. Moreover, Adam and Eve were created in the image of God, so they knew their Father's character, which is revealed in the Ten Commandments. They passed this knowledge to their offspring, but because of man's failing memory, they eventually had to write it down.

CONFESS TO BRETHREN

Must we confess our sins to our Christian brethren in order to be forgiven?

"Confess your trespasses to one another, and pray for one another, that you may be healed. The effective, fervent prayer of a righteous man avails much" (James 5:16).

Principally, all sin is against God and must be confessed only to Him in the closet of prayer. Notice that even after David sinned with Bathsheba and killed Uriah, he prayed, "Against You, You only, have I sinned, and done this evil in Your sight" (Psalm 51:4).

When Achan was identified by God for stealing, his sin was against God *and the people.* Joshua told him, "I beg you, give glory to the LORD God of Israel, and make confession to Him, and tell me now what you have done; do not hide it from me" (Joshua 7:19). Because his sin directly affected the people, or church, he was commanded to acknowledge this publicly. But the confession was to God, not man—because only God can forgive sin. "I, even I, am He who blots out your transgressions for My own sake; and I will not remember your sins" (Isaiah 43:25).

But if we hurt, offend, or abuse another human, whether Christian or pagan, we should acknowledge it and ask them to forgive us. "If you bring your gift to the altar, and there remember that your brother has something against you, leave your gift there before the altar, and go your way. First be reconciled to your brother, and then come and offer your gift" (Matthew 5:23, 24).

Public sin should be acknowledged publicly; offences against individuals should be addressed only with those involved; private sin should be confessed to God privately. Such confession should not be taken lightly. It needs to come from a humble heart. True confession explains what was done. There are no excuses. Paul's example of such specific honesty can be seen in Acts 26:10, 11.

When we genuinely confess our sins to God (and to each other), we will experience God's love and peace. We will be cleansed from unrighteousness.

HEALTHY RELATIONSHIPS

What does the Bible say about dating?

"Do not be unequally yoked together with unbelievers. For what fellowship has righteousness with lawlessness? And what communion has light with darkness?" (2 Corinthians 6:14).

The words "dating" or "courting" aren't found in the Bible, but God's Word does offer principles that can be applied when you're choosing a mate. One of the first considerations for a single Christian is to avoid dating anyone who hasn't accepted Christ. God specifically warns, "Do not be unequally yoked with unbelievers."

If oxen are yoked together for work but one is weaker, they end up going in circles; they can't properly perform their task. A husband and wife are supposed to be a team, but with opposite beliefs they will be at odds. This is likely to cause friction. Furthermore, the Christian in an unequal team can easily drift away from his or her beliefs; over time, the faith of the believer could weaken. For these reasons and others, believers should not marry unbelievers.

The Bible is also clear that any form of pre-marital sex is off limits. Paul writes, "For this is the will of God, your sanctification: that you abstain from sexual immorality; that each one of you know how to control his own body in holiness and honor, not in the passion of lust like the Gentiles who do not know God" (1 Thessalonians 4:3–5).

If you're looking for a mate, put it before the Lord in prayer. God miraculously found a mate for Isaac, Rebecca, Jacob, and many others in the Bible. He will find one for you. "In all your ways acknowledge Him, and He shall direct your paths" (Proverbs 3:6). A consecrated Christian can trust in the Lord to miraculously guide him or her to the right person.

That doesn't mean He doesn't want you to use good judgment, however. Just because you are attracted to someone, for instance, doesn't mean you should marry that person. You need discernment, and God will give you that discernment. If God has someone set up for you, He will give you very powerful evidence that it's the right person.

GOD'S NAME

Does God command us to call Him Jehovah?

"I appeared to Abraham, to Isaac, and to Jacob, as God Almighty, but by My name LORD I was not known to them" *(Exodus 6:3).*

You might have had people come to your door and tell you that "Jehovah" is the only appropriate name to call God. Another group claims that it must be Yahweh, which is the sacred name of God.

But I respectfully disagree with the idea that God desires we call Him by one name over another. In reality, God goes by many names in the Bible. Our text in Exodus does say one of these names is Lord, which is YHWH in Hebrew and often interpreted as Jehovah. However, here God simply revealed a new name to them. And you will find that God continues to reveal new names throughout the Bible. He never says we should use just one name when calling on Him or referencing Him.

Those who become preoccupied with the idea that we must only address God by one name are, in a certain way, making their God smaller. Indeed, God's names tell us about His character. For instance, He also says we should call him Wonderful, Counselor, the Mighty God, and Everlasting Father.

Jesus also has many names: He's called Alpha and Omega, the Lamb, the Beginning and the End, the Gate, the Door, Son of God, and many more. It would be impractical to list them all here! The real issue is not what name we should use when speaking with God, though it should always be done with reverence, holiness, and a sense of awe.

The true issue is whether or not we honor and exalt His Word. Psalm 138:2 says, "You have magnified Your word above all Your name." Indeed, each language has different names to refer to God; but the bona fide uniting force is how God's Word transcends language or simple words and affects all people regardless of the name one chooses to call Him, whether it be Advocate (1 John 2:1), Amen (Revelation 1:8), or Author and Finisher of our faith (Hebrews 12:2).

CHRISTIAN ENTERTAINMENT

What is biblically permissible when it comes to entertainment?

"Whatever things are true, whatever things are noble, whatever things are just, whatever things are pure, whatever things are lovely, whatever things are of good report, if there is any virtue and if there is anything praiseworthy—meditate on these things" (Philippians 4:8).

With the onset of the Internet, smartphones, and HDTVs, the average person swims through a constant waterfall of entertainment advertisements every day. There has never been a time in history when one's senses have been so assaulted by worldly media.

We need to be aware, then, that the Bible standard is very high. In Philippians 4:8, we read, "Whatever things are true, whatever things are noble, whatever things are just ... meditate on these things." If you apply these criteria to what you're watching, reading, and hearing, you will be following the very best counsel available.

King David writes, "I will set nothing wicked before my eyes" (Psalm 101:3). When we follow this as a guideline, we're more likely to choose activities that nurture the fruits of the Spirit in our lives. No one can escape the truth that we are changed by what we behold (see 2 Corinthians 3:18). As we worship and look to Jesus, we become more like Him. As we worship and look to the world, we will become more like the world.

Ultimately, this is the bottom line: "What would Jesus do?" What would He watch, what would He read, and what would He listen to? If He suddenly walked into your room, would you quickly change the channel, slip that novel under your pillow, or delete your browser history? Actually, He and His angels are there now, so these are very good questions to ask yourself in every situation.

A Christian is a follower of Christ, so Jesus' example should be foremost in our minds and hearts. The only way to really find that out is to study to know Him better through your Bible. "Let this mind be in you which was also in Christ Jesus" (Philippians 2:5).

INHERITANCE

Is it proper to leave an inheritance to unconverted children who might squander it?

"An inheritance gained hastily at the beginning will not be blessed at the end" (Proverbs 20:21).

Two facets must be considered when addressing this issue: love for God (loyalty to His cause) and unconditional love for your children.

It is important to communicate love to all our children in our estate planning. If the last act of a parent's life is to cut out a son or daughter from the will, an adult child might be forever turned from accepting the Lord. This leaves a bitter scar that is almost impossible for children to forget. "A good man leaves an inheritance to his children's children" (Proverbs 13:22).

The other dynamic is that we must give an account to God for how we distribute our assets at the time of our deaths. To leave considerable wealth to unconverted children is, for practical purposes, placing God's resources in the devil's hands. "He who loves son or daughter more than Me is not worthy of Me" (Matthew 10:37).

The answer, it seems, is balance. You naturally want to leave enough for your children and grandchildren to communicate your love and thoughtfulness or provide for practical needs such as education. Giving non-cash assets, such as property and family heirlooms, can also convey this.

Before King David died, he told his son Solomon that he arranged to leave the bulk of his assets to build up God's house. "Indeed I have taken much trouble to prepare for the house of the LORD one hundred thousand talents of gold and one million talents of silver, and bronze and iron beyond measure, for it is so abundant" (1 Chronicles 22:14).

You can be sure that David left a generous inheritance for Solomon and all his children, but there is no doubt that the majority of his prosperity went to build up the house of God. This is an excellent example for Christian parents today.

A BIBLICAL DIET

Is vegetarianism biblical?

"For one believes he may eat all things, but he who is weak eats only vegetables. Let not him who eats despise him who does not eat, and let not him who does not eat judge him who eats" (Romans 14:2, 3).

In the New Testament period, there was a debate about whether people should eat animals that had been offered to idols by pagans before being butchered for the marketplace.

Paul advised Christians to ask "no questions for conscience' sake" (1 Corinthians 10:25). But if their conscience bothered them, they could just eat vegetables. It had nothing to do with the benefits of a vegetable diet over a meat diet; it concerned whether or not the meat had been offered to idols.

Salvation is the most important thing here, but in the New Testament, many ceremonial dietary issues got mixed up in the Jews' minds as being moral issues. The apostle Paul advised all believers to be careful not to judge other believers in this regard (Romans 14:3).

While we should never say a person has to be a vegetarian to be saved, the optimal diet should be no surprise. If you want to see God's original intention, you only need look at the creation: "I have given you every herb that yields seed which is on the face of all the earth, and every tree whose fruit yields seed; to you it shall be for food" (Genesis 1:29).

But eventually people developed other appetites—and throughout history, we see that God some- times allows things, because of man's narrow-minded insistence, that are not the best choice.

Science has clearly proven that the original vegetarian diet is far healthier. People tend to live longer on a vegetarian diet; they tend to avoid the diet-related diseases that plague our world. There is also plenty of strength produced from a plant-based diet; many athletes are vegetarians—even some endurance athletes who compete in grueling triathlons.

The original menu God gave humanity will be our diet again when we get to the kingdom. But "whether you eat or drink, or whatever you do, do all to the glory of God" (1 Corinthians 10:31).

Same-Sex Marriage

Should you leave your church if it allows same-sex marriage?

"Adam said: 'This is now bone of my bones and flesh of my flesh; she shall be called Woman, because she was taken out of Man.' Therefore a man shall leave his father and mother and be joined to his wife, and they shall become one flesh" (Genesis 2:23, 24).

Sometimes you might disagree with your church on some trivial difference in doctrine, interpretation, or worship practice—I don't believe these kinds of issues should be an automatic cause of separation. But if a church endorses same-sex marriage, that's something much more serious. The biblical model of marriage is an institution of God, a foundational truth. It is not a trivial matter.

Why? This perversion of marriage is identified in the Bible as an "abomination"—classified as a major sin (Leviticus 20:13). For context, Leviticus 20:15 talks about a man lying down with a beast.

Since we are made in the Creator's image, for a church to endorse same-sex marriage, it openly desecrates the image of God. If they've gone that far, they've drifted into apostasy. While same-sex marriage is now receiving more acceptance in our society, the Bible is very clear: God's Word does not change to fit in with cultural trends.

The Bible defines marriage in concrete terms. From the beginning, God "created them male and female" (Genesis 5:2). He then established marriage. He placed a holy hedge around this institution in order to protect it precisely because it is so valuable, so sacred, so important.

Did you know that the fall of virtually every great empire has been preceded by the disintegration of the family as God defines it? Based on history, if this trend is not reversed, it signals the doom of our nation as well. It's not safe for a church to endorse that, so you might consider calling another church home for a while.

Marriage—in God's definition—can only exist between a man and a woman. We just weren't created for any other arrangement.

JEWISH FESTIVALS

Should Christians observe any of the Jewish festivals?

"Therefore purge out the old leaven, that you may be a new lump, since you truly are unleavened. For indeed Christ, our Passover, was sacrificed for us. Therefore let us keep the feast, not with old leaven, nor with the leaven of malice and wickedness, but with the unleavened bread of sincerity and truth" (1 Corinthians 5:7, 8).

Since Christ is our Passover, we no longer need to sacrifice a Passover lamb; He is that Lamb. This same principal applies to all of the Jewish festivals and feasts. When Christ came and then died on the cross, it changed everything. He was the fulfillment of every type and symbol in the Jewish religious system, whether to things that have happened in the past or will happen in the future.

I have no burden to challenge those who feel convicted to observe these days, but I also don't see the point. I see no reason to keep the Jewish holidays that were a shadow of what Jesus was to do here on earth. Why embrace His shadow when He's before you in flesh and blood? Why stare at a loved one's photo when they're standing next to you? Some feasts required worshipers to offer sacrifices at the Jerusalem temple, so it's obviously not possible to keep them now.

The festivals remembering the Exodus and the sanctuary were "nailed to the cross" when Jesus died (Colossians 2:16). They were shadows (v. 17), the handwriting of ordinances on paper. In contrast, the unchanging Sabbath was written in stone. That is why the temple veil was ripped from top to bottom in Matthew 27:51. No man could have ripped that veil in that fashion. It was an indication from God that the types that pointed to Jesus ended with the crucifixion. Daniel 9:27 prophesies this when it says, "Then he shall confirm a covenant with many for one week; but in the middle of the week He shall bring an end to sacrifice and offering."

In the place of the Passover, Jesus gave us the communion service; the national festival of the Jews was to pass away.

Jesus' Family

Are there any Bible verses that say
Joseph was previously married or had
children before he married Mary?

"'Is this not the carpenter, the Son of Mary, and brother of James, Joses, Judas, and Simon? And are not His sisters here with us?' So they were offended at Him" (Mark 6:3).

No Scripture says that Joseph had children before Mary, but we can come to that conclusion through some simple detective work. For instance, the Bible tells us in several places that Jesus had brothers and sisters. When Jesus was dying on the cross, He committed the care of His mother to the apostle John (John 19:25–27). That would have been a very unusual act if the other children had been her offspring. She would have automatically been under their care if that were the case.

Furthermore, during the time of Jesus, it was the duty of the oldest son in a family to stay home and work with the father to eventually take over his business. If Jesus had been the eldest, it would have been an insult to leave Joseph in the carpenter shop and go off preaching. But because Jesus was one of the younger sons, it wasn't a problem.

When we put these things together, it makes sense that Jesus was not Joseph's first son. You typically hear about Mary and Joseph and Jesus' brothers and sisters. However, it seems Joseph had died by the time Christ began His ministry, so scholars conclude that he was older than Mary and had already had a family before marrying her. His first wife had evidently passed away, and Joseph himself is never mentioned as being alive when Christ began His ministry.

A lot of this comes from simple deduction. Joseph died from old age and/or hard work by the time Jesus began His ministry. The older brothers of Christ continued working in the carpenter shop in Nazareth, and Jesus was Mary's only biological son as far as we can tell.

What is most important is that we know and believe that Jesus was the Son of God. Our passage today suggests the people in His hometown of Nazareth rejected Him. Will you receive Him?

THE OLD COVENANT

Wasn't the old covenant the Ten Commandments?

"If that first covenant had been faultless, then no place would have been sought for a second. Because finding fault with them, He says: 'Behold, the days are coming, says the LORD, when I will make a new covenant with the house of Israel and with the house of Judah'" (Hebrews 8:7, 8).

The question of the covenants has been greatly distorted and misunderstood. Let's begin by noticing what the old covenant was *not*. It was not the Ten Commandments. Why? Because God's eternal law did not grow old and vanish away (v. 13). They did not have poor promises (v. 6), and they were not faulty (v. 7).

Then what was the old covenant, and how was it ratified? It was an agreement between God and Israel. When Moses shared the covenant with Israel, they replied, "All that the LORD has spoken we will do" (Exodus 19:8). The people promised to keep the Ten Commandments. It was ratified by the sprinkled blood of an ox (Exodus 24:7, 8). The promises of the people failed because they tried to obey in their human strength alone.

In comparison, the new covenant was instituted and ratified by the blood of Jesus at His death (Hebrews 12:24; 13:20; Matthew 26:28). It went into effect when He died. "For a testament (covenant) is in force after men are dead, since it had no power at all while the testator lives" (Hebrews 9:17).

In speaking of the new covenant, the apostle Paul writes: "Though it is only a man's covenant, yet if it is confirmed, no one annuls or adds to it" (Galatians 3:15). This means that after the death of Christ, nothing could be added to or taken away from the new covenant. Jesus introduced the Lord's Supper on Thursday night before He died, so it came under the new covenant (Matthew 26:28).

Here's a question worth asking: "When did Sunday-keeping begin?" Everyone answers, "After the resurrection." If that is the case, then it cannot be part of the new covenant since it took place *after* the death of Jesus. Can anything be "added" after the death of Jesus, the testator?

Some Christians believe that the Ten Commandment law was only a part of the law of Moses, which disappeared with the old covenant. These verses in Hebrews 10 are used to support this premise. The "law" of verse 8 is undoubtedly associated with the "first" covenant, which is taken away in verse 9.

But did that law include the Ten Commandments? Those same sacrifices and sin offerings are described in 2 Chronicles 8:12, 13, when Solomon offered burnt offerings "according to the commandment of Moses."

This makes it plain that the law concerning those burnt offerings—the one mentioned in Hebrews 10:8—was called the commandment or law of Moses. It was part of the old covenant system that was taken away by "the offering of the body of Jesus Christ" (verse 10). But note: The Ten Commandments were not part of that. Christ is quoted in verse 9, saying, " 'Behold, I have come to do Your will, O God.' He takes away the first that He may establish the second."

The full text of what Christ said comes from Psalm 40:8, which says, "I delight to do Your will, O my God, and Your law is within my heart." This law is tied to the second (or new) covenant that was to be established. This is reinforced a few verses later in Hebrews 10, where it says, "This is the covenant that I will make with them after those days, says the LORD: I will put My laws into their hearts, and in their minds I will write them" (v. 16).

The law that was in the heart of Jesus and which did not end with the old covenant is the Ten Commandment law. Magnified by Christ (Isaiah 42:21), it was transferred from the tables of stone to the tables of the heart.

The Bible says, "If that first covenant had been faultless, then no place would have been sought for a second" (Hebrews 8:7). So let me ask you: Has any man been able to find a flaw in the handwriting of God? The psalmist declared, "The law of the LORD is perfect, converting the soul" (Psalm 19:7).

Romans 7:12 adds, "The law is holy, and the commandment holy and just and good." Does that sound like something weak and imperfect? No law could be perfect *and* faulty at the same time. It becomes quite apparent that the old covenant could not have been the Ten Commandments themselves; instead, the Commandments were the terms of the covenant, not the actual covenant.

The word "covenant" means agreement—at fault with this first agreement was the promise of the people, "All the LORD has said we will do." The new covenant is the same law, but written by the Lord on the human heart. "This is the covenant that I will make with the house of Israel after those days, says the LORD: I will put My law in their minds, and write it on their hearts; and I will be their God" (Jeremiah 31:33). Notice, it is the same law you find in the Ten Commandments, but now it's written in the heart. Indeed, the new covenant goes even deeper than the letter of the law—it goes to the spirit of the law.

Jesus illustrated this when He said, "You have heard that it was said to those of old, 'You shall not murder, and whoever murders will be in danger of the judgment.' But I say to you that whoever is angry with his brother without a cause shall be in danger of the judgment" (Matthew 5:21, 22).

Jesus taught us that the new covenant is not based on merely obeying the Ten Commandments, but also the attitude behind our deeds. The change of heart will lead to the change of life.

Jewelry

Doesn't the ring on the finger of the prodigal son support the wearing of jewelry?

"The father said to his servants, 'Bring out the best robe and put it on him, and put a ring on his hand and sandals on his feet'" (Luke 15:22).

A vital principle of Bible study is to seek to understand the meaning and purpose behind a passage of Scripture. Using one verse to prove a point that was never intended does injustice to the Word of God. So we need to ask, "What is the message of this text?" Some have used this Scripture to justify the wearing of jewelry, but like all parables, this story teaches us about spiritual realities.

God is here represented as welcoming home one of His lost children. The prodigal "came to himself" (v. 17) and returns home to the heavenly Father. The welcome he received describes how God treats us when we return to Him.

There are three things the father does for his returning son. He puts the best robe on him (which implies his own robe), he puts a ring on his hand, and he puts sandals on his feet. The best robe is a beautiful illustration of how Christ covers us with His pure righteousness. We all come in filthy rags. Sandals were worn only by members of a household; servants couldn't afford shoes. The Lord tells us here, "You are part of My family again."

So what does a ring on the son's finger mean? Did the father simply want his son to look nice? No. It meant much more. It was probably a signet ring, which represented the authority to transact business for the family. The level to which the father raised this prodigal son is astounding; it probably shocked the people who first heard Christ tell this story.

The ring had nothing to do with whether or not we should wear jewelry. It's a stretch to use this text to support decorating our bodies with ornaments. It's better for us to study all of what Scripture says about how God's remnant people dress to prepare for Christ's coming than to squeeze a questionable point out of this verse.

SHROUD OF TURIN

Is the Shroud of Turin a real biblical artifact?

"They took the body of Jesus, and bound it in strips of linen with the spices" (John 19:40).

While this isn't really about the Bible, it remains a popular question about Jesus that needs some attention.

The Shroud is a long strip of linen bearing the image of a man who appears to have suffered physical trauma consistent with a crucifixion. Many believe this is the actual cloth used to embalm Jesus.

I don't believe that this shroud has anything to do with Jesus. The Bible says that His body was bound in strips of linen with spices (John 19:40), more like a mummy, and that a separate napkin was wrapped around His head (John 20:5–7). The Shroud of Turin, on the other hand, is a single cloth that was folded up the front and down the back of the individual's body.

A few years ago, the first scientific tests suggested that it did date back to the time of Christ and that it originated in Palestine. For example, they found pollen particles on it that were native only to Palestine. Later, different researchers announced that the cloth dated back only to about AD 1300. Now the University of Padua claims that the shroud dates between 300 BC and AD 400. Other research has concluded that the stains on the cloth are not from blood.

Around the time the Shroud first appeared, there were many other "true" shrouds also appearing around Europe. At least 43 "true shrouds" circulated in medieval Europe after the Crusades, which brought lots of supposed "relics" from the east. In fact, you can still travel Europe and see some of these shrouds. Tellingly, no burial garments from the time of Christ resemble the Shroud of Turin.

The Shroud might have been the result of a crucifixion, as Muslims punished some of the Crusaders by crucifying them. Either way, we know the Lord does not want us worshiping relics, true or false. When the children of Israel began to pray and burn incense before the bronze serpent Moses had made, King Hezekiah crushed it into powder.

Parables

Did Jesus purposely use parables to frustrate people who sought to be converted?

"To you it has been given to know the mystery of the kingdom of God; but to those who are outside, all things come in parables, so that 'Seeing they may see and not perceive, and hearing they may hear and not understand; lest they should turn, and their sins be forgiven them'" (Mark 4:11, 12).

Some have read this text and wondered if Christ used parables to deliberately confuse certain people who might otherwise have been converted. Like many Bible questions, it is best to look at other verses to see what God says about His desire for people to be saved. See Revelation 22:17, for instance, which makes it plain that "whosoever desires" may come to and be accepted into the kingdom.

The apostle Peter stated, "The Lord is not slack concerning His promise, as some count slackness, but is longsuffering toward us, not willing that any should perish but that all should come to repentance" (2 Peter 3:9). It is clear through other Bible writers that God never intended to hide any truth that would lead a person to repentance and conversion.

So what does this passage in Mark really mean? The verse is made clear by reading a parallel account in Matthew's gospel, when a reason is given why some people do not hear or see the truth. "For the hearts of this people have grown dull. Their ears are hard of hearing, and their eyes they have closed, lest they should see with their eyes and hear with their ears, lest they should understand with their hearts and turn, so that I should heal them" (Matthew 13:15).

Christ's words are spoken in irony. Another way of saying this verse might be, "These people plug their ears and refuse to listen! They squeeze their eyes shut and cannot see anything." Zechariah describes some people who turn from God by saying, "Yes, they made their hearts like flint, refusing to hear the law" (Zechariah 7:12).

Jesus wisely used parables to bypass prejudiced minds. But for those who insisted on refusing to hear His words, the parables were meaningless and only "increased" their darkness. May it not be so for you and me!

GROWING IN FAITH

How can I make my faith in God stronger?

"Now faith is the substance of things hoped for, the evidence of things not seen" (Hebrews 11:1).

Faith is a word we don't always use in our everyday vocabulary. It's often relegated to the field of theology. But actually, faith is the foundation of our daily walk with God. Simply put—it's trusting in the Lord. Every time you sit in a chair, you have "faith" that it will hold you up and not collapse beneath you. Faith is trusting that God will hold us up through the thick and the thin.

Many people have strong faith when everything is going well in their lives, but when a storm comes through, they lose their grip on God. It reminds me of a simple illustration from the field of aviation. As a pilot, one of the expressions I'll sometimes use is "flying blind." It simply means that when your outside visuals are obliterated by clouds, bad weather, or darkness, you fly the airplane solely by relying on the instruments. It's a bit scary when you first learn how to trust what's on the panel in front of you and not worry about the darkness outside. But without it, you are destined to crash and burn!

Exercising trust in God when things are dark and gloomy helps our faith grow strong. As we develop a relationship with Jesus through daily Bible study and prayer, we learn that He truly loves us and has our best interests in mind. "For I know the thoughts that I think toward you, says the LORD, thoughts of peace and not of evil, to give you a future and a hope" (Jeremiah 29:11). The more we come to know of God's love, the more we'll trust Him.

Every Christian is given a measure of faith by God (Romans 12:3). It's amazing what even a little faith can do. Jesus said, "If you have faith as a mustard seed, you will say to this mountain, 'Move from here to there,' and it will move; and nothing will be impossible for you" (Matthew 17:20).

PRIVATE BAPTISM

Is having a private baptism without a pastor present biblically valid?

"Therefore, brethren, seek out from among you seven men of good reputation, full of the Holy Spirit and wisdom, whom we may appoint over this business" (Acts 6:3).

The people who baptized in Bible times were men who had been commissioned by God and given authority: the prophets, John the Baptist, and the apostles, for example. The Bible seems to establish this as a precedent.

Acts 6:3 says that when the apostles set up the office of deacon, they chose seven men who were "of good reputation" and "full of the Holy Spirit and wisdom." Then, to make it official, these men were set before the apostles, who prayed and laid hands on them (v. 6). When Philip baptized the Ethiopian eunuch (Acts 8:26–39), we don't know if he was still a deacon or if he had been "promoted." We do know, however, that there is no record in the Bible of the disciples baptizing one another.

Let me tell you why I think that is. I'm a pastor, and if all of my church members believed they could go out and baptize whomever they felt led to baptize, without any kind of clearing process, they could wind up bringing people into the church who had not really been taught. Jesus said, "Go therefore and make disciples of all the nations, baptizing them in the name of the Father and of the Son and of the Holy Spirit, *teaching them to observe all things that I have commanded you*" (Matthew 28:19, 20, my emphasis).

I'm not going to be dogmatic and say that God would not honor a private baptism at which no pastor is present. There have been Christians in communist countries who accepted Jesus and then baptized each other. But they were operating under extreme circumstances. Insofar as possible, baptism should be a *public* declaration of our decision to follow Christ.

If you have Bible-teaching churches in your community that teach and practice baptism by immersion, why wouldn't you want to participate in a public baptism and invite your pastor?

TRINITY

What is the nature of the Trinity?

"As the heavens are higher than the earth, so are My ways higher than your ways, and My thoughts than your thoughts" *(Isaiah 55:9).*

This subject has been debated by the great minds of Christendom for nearly 2,000 years. When mortals try to describe God, all we can do is make our best attempt. If we could reach the farthest stars, maybe we could explain God. But we can't. The Bible does, however, tell us enough so we don't have to doubt.

God is a unit of three persons. "God" is a family word; He consists of God the Father, God the Son, and God the Holy Spirit. In John 3:16, we see that God the Father sent God the Son in the form of a human that we might be forgiven. At Jesus' baptism, you see these individuals again. The Father speaks from heaven saying, "This is my beloved son." Then the Spirit comes down in the form of a dove upon the Son. You've got the Father, the Son, and the Holy Spirit all right there.

Some people are confused because Moses says, "Hear, O Israel: The LORD our God, the LORD is one!" (Deuteronomy 6:4). But the Bible also tells us, "God said, 'Let Us make man in Our image'" (Genesis 1:26).

The word "one" in the Bible doesn't just mean one person; it can also mean one in unity or in purpose. Speaking of the apostles, Jesus prayed "that they all may be one, as You, Father, are in Me, and I in You; that they also may be one in Us" (John 17:21). Galatians 4:4–6 says, "God sent forth His Son…that we might receive the adoption as sons. And because you are sons, God has sent forth the Spirit of His Son into your hearts, crying out, 'Abba, Father!'" Here you have God the Father sending the Son and sending the Spirit that we might reflect God the Son. There are many different titles used in the Bible for God, but there is only one God who is united in His purpose of saving you and me. That's the Trinity.

TEN COMMANDMENTS ABOLISHED?

Weren't the Ten Commandments part of the old covenant that was abolished at the cross?

"So He declared to you His covenant which He commanded you to perform, the Ten Commandments; and He wrote them on two tablets of stone" (Deuteronomy 4:13).

Some Christians teach that the Ten Commandments are a core part of the old covenant, which was abolished. Yet even though the Ten Commandments were indeed a commanded covenant, they did not constitute the old covenant that vanished away (Hebrews 8:13). Here are some reasons:

1. The old covenant was faulty, had poor promises, and vanished away (Hebrews 8:7, 8, 13). None of those points apply to the perfect law of God (Psalm 19:7).

2. The old covenant was made based on the Israelites' promise to keep God's commandments in their own strength (Exodus 24:7, 8). It was not the law itself.

3. Referring to the Ten Commandments, God said to Moses, "According to the tenor of these words I have made a covenant with you and with Israel" (Exodus 34:27, 28). It was not the law itself but the promise to keep the law.

4. Moses referred to the golden calf as "your sin, the calf which you had made" (Deuteronomy 9:21). The calf was not the sin, but the sin took place concerning the calf. In the same way, the old covenant was not the law, but it was *concerning* the law. Thus it is called the covenant.

5. Romans 9:4 shows that the old and new covenants were different from the law itself: "...who are Israelites, to whom pertain the adoption, the glory, the covenants, the giving of the law, the service of God, and the promises." Here the law is listed, as well as the covenants (plural). This would include both old and new covenants, plus the "giving of the law," which are the Ten Commandments.

6. To demonstrate how the law is not the old covenant, let's interchange some words in Romans 3:31 and see what happens: "Do we then make void the (old covenant) through faith? Certainly not! On the contrary, we establish the (old covenant)." That obviously doesn't make much sense, does it?

Going to the Movies

Is it bad for a Christian to see a good movie?

"Whatever things are true, whatever things are noble, whatever things are just, whatever things are pure, whatever things are lovely, whatever things are of good report, if there is any virtue and if there is anything praiseworthy—meditate on these things" (Philippians 4:8).

What we put into our minds is extremely important as it affects our spiritual lives. The vast majority of movies do not fit the Bible's criteria of what we should allow into our minds. Many movies that are considered "good" movies have themes that are contrary to the Bible and Christian life.

Scripture tells us that we "beholding as in a mirror the glory of the Lord, are being transformed into the same image" (2 Corinthians 3:18). Looking at Christ makes us more like Christ, but the opposite applies as well. What we look at has a definite effect on our thoughts, beliefs, motivations, goals, and characters. Most movies feature violence, sexual content, and foul language—things that Christians should steer away from. None of this can help us become more like Christ.

But suppose there is an innocent, G-rated film that you would like to see. What's wrong with going to the theater to watch it? There are a couple of things you might want to consider. First, if you go to a G-rated movie, you will still expose yourself to advertisements and previews that are not so wholesome, and you might be tempted to come back and see a bad movie. In other words, it opens the door for compromise.

Also, as a Christian, you want to set a good example for others. If someone you know sees you going into a theater, they don't know what movie you're there to see. They could actually use your mere presence at the cinema as an excuse to attend another movie of their choice. The apostle Paul put it this way: "Therefore let us not judge one another anymore, but rather resolve this, not to put a stumbling block or a cause to fall in our brother's way" (Romans 14:13).

Vain Repetition in Prayer

Where is the line between persisting in prayer and vain repetition?

"When you pray, do not use vain repetitions as the heathen do. For they think that they will be heard for their many words. Therefore do not be like them. For your Father knows the things you have need of before you ask Him" (Matthew 6:7, 8).

Prayer is not for informing God; rather, it draws us up to God. The Lord wants us to pray to Him for our benefit, and not because He wouldn't know what's going on if we didn't pray. It binds us to God. He knows what you need even before you ask, so the Lord lays certain burdens on our heart, and as long as those burdens are there, we should keep praying for them.

The heathen would utter the same prayer several times in one sitting. That's not prayer. Prayer is the intelligent cry of your heart to the heart of God. Prayer elevates you. When you pray, you should think about the prayer and what you're saying really means.

The Greek word for "vain repetitions" is only found in this one place in the New Testament. It means "to babble" and to "rattle off without giving much thought to what is being said." Is this how Jesus wants us to pray? What follows in verses 9–13 is a simple example of how we might pray. But it's not intended to be a magic formula that will do wonders if we vainly repeat it.

There are some Christian denominations that tell people that when they sin, they should say a certain prayer over and over again in order to right the wrong they did. That's not biblical.

Then you've got people like Elijah who knelt down and, seven times, asked God to send the rain. I don't think he prayed the exact same prayer seven times. Rather, seven different times he pled with the Lord to fulfill His Word and send the rain. People who have children wandering from God pray for their salvation every day. That's not praying in vain repetition. You can be sure that Jesus prayed for the disciples every day (John 17).

ANGER

What are some biblical tips to dealing with personal anger?

"There is no creature hidden from His sight, but all things are naked and open to the eyes of Him to whom we must give account" (Hebrews 4:13).

The first step for dealing with any bad habit or sin is to acknowledge it. When you admit to yourself and to God that you have a problem with anger, you've taken a big step. Being honest with God is necessary if you're going to deal with this issue.

Some people don't see their anger as a problem. While everyone, at some time or another, gets upset, this emotion can lead to some serious consequences. Paul writes, "'Be angry, and do not sin': do not let the sun go down on your wrath, nor give place to the devil" (Ephesians 4:26, 27). If we do not handle our anger properly, it gives Satan a foothold into our lives.

You might even feel that you have a right to be angry, but if it continues to live in your heart, it will eventually destroy you. "So then, my beloved brethren, let every man be swift to hear, slow to speak, slow to wrath; for the wrath of man does not produce the righteousness of God" (James 1:19, 20). Jesus also warned, "I say to you that whoever is angry with his brother without a cause shall be in danger of the judgment" (Matthew 5:22).

Ask yourself, "Why am I angry?" You might be allowing other people to control you and need to draw boundaries with them. It might be that you've genuinely been hurt and need to work something through. But as you deal with your anger, don't let your emotions completely take control of your thinking. "He who is slow to anger is better than the mighty, and he who rules his spirit than he who takes a city" (Proverbs 16:32).

Turn your anger over to God in prayer (Proverbs 15:1). Forgive people who have wounded you (Ephesians 4:32). Ask God to forgive you for treating others poorly when you are angry (1 John 1:9). And don't let it grow into a root of bitterness that will defile you and others around you (Hebrews 12:15).

WOMEN IN MINISTRY

What does the Bible say about women as church leaders or preachers?

"Now there was one, Anna, a prophetess.... She was of a great age, and had lived with a husband seven years from her virginity; and this woman was a widow of about eighty-four years, who did not depart from the temple, but served God with fastings and prayers night and day" (Luke 2:36, 37).

God made men and women as equal creatures. I do not believe there is a distinction between men and women in their value to God and their accessibility to salvation. They're both perfectly equal.

Furthermore, God ministers through both men and women. You read in the Bible about both men and women teaching and preaching, in the capacity of prophets and evangelists, or giving Bible studies, as Priscilla did with her husband, Aquila (Acts 18:26). However, there is no example in the Bible of a woman serving in the capacity of priest, pastor, or elder.

When Jesus chose the 12 disciples, I do not believe He was merely accommodating the traditions of the day when He selected only men. Several offices have uniquely male symbolism. For example, the men were to be the priests of their families. That means servant-leaders, not dictators or despots. Consider Moses' family: Amram and Jochebed had three children: Miriam, Aaron, and Moses. All three were prophets. Their sons both served as priests, but Miriam did not. She was a prophetess, but not a priest. She led the women in prophetic songs and in teaching.

You've read about Anna in the temple (Luke 2:36, 37) and Deborah as a prophetess and a judge in Israel (Judges 4:4), but you've never read of women offering a sacrifice. In the Bible, a priest is a male role because he symbolizes Jesus, our High Priest. A similar distinction was made for the Passover sacrifice. The Israelites were instructed to take a male lamb because it was a symbol for Christ.

God has distinctions in the genders and in roles within the family. I don't think these identities evaporate when people walk through the doors of the church, which is really an extension of the individual family unit.

CULTS

How do you differentiate between opinion and
fact when it comes to discerning between Bible-
believing churches and off-the-wall cults?

"Test all things; hold fast what is good" (1 Thessalonians 5:21).

The answer to this is really quite simple. When prayerfully and
faithfully comparing Scriptures to one another, you'll see the
picture God wants you to see. It's like putting a puzzle together
piece by piece. If you have to jam pieces into place, you're doing
something wrong. They should fit easily together; there's searching
involved, yes, but you shouldn't have to force the text. We must let the
Bible interpret itself.

So Bible-believing churches should base their conclusions on what
the Bible says, without allowing an individual or group of people to
interpret everything for its members. Several members should study
the Bible and bounce ideas off one another. The Bible says, "In the
multitude of counselors there is safety" (Proverbs 11:14).

Cults are classified as such because an elite person or inner circle
does all the thinking for the followers—even when members disagree,
they can't challenge or take a stand against the leadership. People who
blindly follow this kind of practice without Bible study are in danger
of being lost!

A cult also forbids members from looking at outside literature.
Some have come knocking on my door wanting to study the Bible with
me. They are almost always sincere, and I admire their enthusiasm.
But before they leave, I offer them a book. Yet they won't dare take
it, because their church is afraid that their doctrines won't stand up
under scrutiny. A challenge to the church is forbidden.

The Bible says, "Beloved, do not believe every spirit, but test the
spirits, whether they are of God; because many false prophets have
gone out into the world" (1 John 4:1). We ought to prove all things, so
we need to keep our eyes open. You don't need to look at garbage, but
you must examine and evaluate truth, holding fast to the good. With
heartfelt prayer and study, God will lead you.

RETIREMENT

If we believe Jesus is coming soon, is it a lack of faith for us to prepare for retirement?

"He called ten of his servants, delivered to them ten minas, and said to them, 'Do business till I come'" (Luke 19:13).

Planning for retirement doesn't represent a lack of faith. I believe Christians should have a relationship with the Lord in which they remember they could die at any moment or that Jesus could come at any time, yet plan for the future as though this planet could last another hundred years.

Jesus told a parable in Luke 19:12–27 about a ruler who went away on a long trip but promised to return. Before he left, the man called 10 of his servants and gave them a very large sum of money. His parting instructions were, "Do business till I come" (v. 13). In other words, Jesus was telling His disciples to stay busy, invest, and plan for the future.

For example, if you're going to build a house, don't build it to last only five years even if you believe the Lord is coming soon. My advice is to dig deep and build your foundation well. The Bible says, "Whatever your hand finds to do, do it with your might" (Ecclesiastes 9:10).

I once heard a story that helps to illustrate this point. A young monk living in a monastery was reading some of the Scriptures chained to the wall that told about the imminence of Christ's coming. He got very excited and ran out to St. Francis, who was harvesting peas in the garden. The young monk exclaimed, "Jesus is coming!"

"Yes, my son," St. Francis replied.

"He's coming soon," emphasized the young man.

Saint Francis acknowledged, "I know, my son."

"Well," asked the monk, "how can you just stand there and harvest your peas? What if He was coming tomorrow? What would you be doing now?"

"Well, first I'd finish harvesting the peas," St. Francis answered.

That's the attitude I think Christians should have. Be faithful in what lies closest to you, because we don't know the day or the hour of Jesus' return (Mark 13:32–33).

PENTECOST

What day of the week was Pentecost?

"You shall count seven weeks for yourself; begin to count the seven weeks from the time you begin to put the sickle to the grain" (Deuteronomy 16:9).

Pentecost, also called the Feast of Weeks (Leviticus 23:15–21), occurred on what we would call Sunday and was a celebration of the spring harvest. The root word "pente" means five; for example, a pentagon has five sides. After Passover, there are seven weeks, and after the last Passover Sabbath, which is the 49th day, comes the day of Pentecost. The word literally means "fiftieth day."

Unfortunately, some people use this ceremonial day as a justification for going to church on Sunday, ignoring the Sabbath of the fourth commandment. But that is quite a stretch. There is nothing in the Bible that says to keep Pentecost, Sunday, or even the day of Jesus' resurrection holy as a replacement for the seventh-day Sabbath.

By that logic, we could keep Thursday as the Sabbath because that's when the Lord instituted the New Covenant at the Lord's Supper. You could even argue that it should be Friday, because that's when Jesus was crucified.

But nowhere in the Bible does God pick any other day to replace the seventh day. I think it's pretty reckless for Christians to start altering the law of God, the one He spoke with His voice and wrote with His finger. Jesus said, "Why do you also transgress the commandment of God because of your tradition?" (Matthew 15:3).

If you can show me a Scripture that says, "Keep the first day as the Sabbath," then I'll do just that. But until I find it, should I take men's traditions over the very clear Word of God? The Bible says that the Lord blessed and sanctified the *seventh* day. He wrote it in stone with His finger; He spoke it with His voice, saying, "Remember," meaning that we're not to forget it. We can't simply ignore the Word of God. "And in vain they worship Me, teaching as doctrines the commandments of men" (Matthew 15:9).

SIN

Can you think a sin?

"You have heard that it was said to those of old, 'You shall not murder, and whoever murders will be in danger of the judgment.' But I say to you that whoever is angry with his brother without a cause shall be in danger of the judgment. And whoever says to his brother, 'Raca!' shall be in danger of the council. But whoever says, 'You fool!' shall be in danger of hell fire" (Matthew 5:21, 22).

Let's see what Jesus says about sin in the mind. In Matthew 5:21, our Lord says, "You have heard that it was said to those of old, 'You shall not murder, and whoever murders will be in danger of the judgment.' But I say to you that whoever is angry with his brother without a cause shall be in danger of the judgment." I don't believe He's actually calling someone like this a murderer; rather, He's discussing the significance of thinking angry thoughts.

Now jump down to verses 27 and 28. "You have heard that it was said to those of old, 'You shall not commit adultery.' But I say to you that whoever looks at a woman to lust for her has already committed adultery with her in his heart." Here the Lord is telling us that sin is not always an action; it can be an attitude. It can be a thought.

On another occasion, Jesus explained, "For from within, out of the heart of man, come evil thoughts, sexual immorality, theft, murder, adultery, coveting, wickedness, deceit, sensuality, envy, slander, pride, foolishness. All these evil things come from within, and they defile a person" (Mark 7:21–23). Our minds are where all sin begins.

In the Sermon on the Mount, Jesus spent a lot more time talking about the attitude of pride and arrogance and sinful thoughts than the actual deeds, because every sinful deed originates with a thought in the mind. So if we're going to squelch sin in our lives, we need to begin by asking the Lord to bring our minds and our thoughts into captivity to His Holy Spirit.

The Sabbath

Which day is the Sabbath and does it still matter today?

*"But the seventh day is the Sabbath of the LORD your God.
... For in six days the LORD made the heavens and the earth,
the sea, and all that is in them, and rested the seventh day"
(Exodus 20:10, 11).*

The Bible is very clear that the Sabbath is the seventh day of the week. Many spiritual people worship Jesus on the first day of the week (Sunday), believing that the Sabbath was meant for the Jews only. But is this true? Genesis 2:1, 2 shows us that God established the Sabbath as a memorial of creation. No Jews existed at the beginning of the world! God chose a day to remind not only the Jews, but all of humanity, that He is both our sustainer and our Creator.

How do we know that the seventh day is what we call "Saturday"? First of all, Jews today still worship on Saturday. For a whole nation to forget which day is the Sabbath would be hard to believe! Second, astronomers who have studied changes in the calendar affirm that while many changes to the calendar have been made, they in no way affected the weekly cycle.

Third, the Bible tells us that even in His death, Jesus rested on the Sabbath. He was crucified on a Friday, the preparation day; He rested in the tomb on the Sabbath; and He rose the first day of the week. Fourth, dictionaries define "Sunday" as the first day of the week and "Saturday" as the seventh day. Indeed, if one looks at a calendar, the weeks begin with Sunday and end with Saturday. Fifth, in 145 languages of the world, the word for the seventh day of the week means "Sabbath day"!

God knew we needed a special day on which to nurture our relationship with Him. The devil wants us to forget about that time of rest so that our relationship with God will be destroyed. However, God still calls us to "Remember the Sabbath day" (Exodus 20:8) and honor Him as Creator by setting it apart for Him each week.

BAPTISM

Must a person first overcome every bad habit before being baptized?

"Therefore bear fruits worthy of repentance" (Matthew 3:8).

I believe that certain tangible life changes should be evident before baptism. This is why John the Baptist stated, "Bear fruits worthy of repentance" (Matthew 3:8). Since baptism reflects new birth, new life, and liberation from a life of sin, being baptized while still enslaved to sinful habits, such as drinking, would be a paradox.

Baptism is similar to marriage. For a man to marry a woman while still dating another would be a lie. Similarly, a person shouldn't enter into a union with Christ through baptism while willingly still "dating the devil" in certain areas of life.

When people are baptized, they are publicly renouncing their old life of sin. Remember that baptism symbolizes death to the old way of life. When a person comes up out of the water, it is a symbol of resurrection and new life in Christ. The Bible says, "Therefore we were buried with Him through baptism into death, that just as Christ was raised from the dead by the glory of the Father, even so we also should walk in newness of life" (Romans 6:4).

I am not suggesting that an individual needs to know everything or should be perfect before baptism. There isn't anyone who meets those criteria. However, no one should enter into this special relationship unrepentant. To repent means to turn away from doing wrong and determine to do what is right with God's help. The Word of God puts it this way: "Knowing this, that our old man was crucified with Him, that the body of sin might be done away with, that we should no longer be slaves of sin" (Romans 6:6). Evidence of Christ's victory will be apparent in a life that is consecrated to the Lord.

Of course, baptism does not bring perfection, and new believers will certainly feel a need for repentance after baptism. Thankfully, we have the promise that "if anyone sins, we have an Advocate with the Father, Jesus Christ the righteous" (1 John 2:1). As we go to Him daily, asking for forgiveness and the power to do His will, we will grow to be more like our Savior.

SABBATH WORK

Are some types of work permissible on Sabbath, such as nursing?

"What man is there among you who has one sheep, and if it falls into a pit on the Sabbath, will not lay hold of it and lift it out? Of how much more value then is a man than a sheep? Therefore it is lawful to do good on the Sabbath" (Matthew 12:11, 12).

The Bible records that Jesus, by His example, showed that it is righteous to relieve suffering on the Sabbath.

In one instance, Jesus was teaching in a synagogue on Sabbath and there was a crippled woman present. She had a "spirit of infirmity" and had been bent over and unable to straighten herself for 18 years. Jesus called to her and told her she was loosed from her infirmity. Then "He laid His hands on her, and immediately she was made straight, and glorified God" (Luke 13:13). The Bible records several more instances in which people were healed by Jesus on the Sabbath. Just before healing a man with a withered hand, Jesus stated, "It is lawful to do good on the Sabbath" (Matthew 12:12).

By relieving the afflicted, we bring honor to His day. However, we are not to do unnecessary work or anything that can be done another day. Because of the nature of nursing duties, some are tempted to feel justified in doing things on the Sabbath that aren't necessary. This can become habitual, until the sense of Sabbath sacredness is lost and God's commandments are broken.

Some people in the medical field perform services on the Sabbath so they will be free other days of the week to do their own thing. That, I believe, is consciously breaking God's commandment. Yet there are times when we must take our turn, and emergencies can arise when we must do our healing duties on the Sabbath. Some conscientious Christians even put the money they make on those days into God's treasury, and I believe God honors and blesses these.

Whatever your situation, God will guide you if you put your trust in Him (Proverbs 3:5, 6).

THE BIBLE

When was the Bible first published?

"Heaven and earth will pass away, but My words will by no means pass away" (Matthew 24:35).

The Bible was first mass printed in the mid-15th century, when Johann Gutenberg invented a new form of movable type that eventually led to the mass production of books. The Gutenberg Bible was published in Mainz, Germany, around AD 1454, and it was the first major book printed in the West. About 180 copies were made, and significant parts of 48 copies still remain.

However, the Bible was preserved and duplicated for many centuries before Gutenberg published it. The books of the Old Testament existed before Jesus was born, and both He and His disciples called them "the law and the prophets" (Luke 16:16).

The Jews guarded the Old Testament Scriptures so carefully that if a scribe made a single mistake while making a copy, he had to destroy the entire manuscript! It was a life's work to ensure that every letter was just right, and curses were pronounced on any scribe who dared alter God's Word in any way. This careful work paid off. The text of the Dead Sea Scrolls, which existed before the time of Christ, is almost exactly like the versions of the Old Testament we have today.

After Jesus died, Mark, Matthew, Luke, and John penned their Gospels and Paul wrote his letters. Many years later, godly men began to assemble all of the writings from after the time of Christ, which they referred to as the New Testament. By AD 300, all of these books had been compiled to form the Bible that we still use today. The original language of the Old Testament is Hebrew and some Aramaic, whereas the New Testament was written in Greek.

The Greek word for Bible (*biblia*) means "books," which accurately describes the collection of 66 sacred texts. God moved on the hearts of people, who were inspired by the Holy Spirit, to write down in human language truths impressed upon them for the purpose of spreading God's message of salvation to others. Today, the Bible is the bestselling book of all time. About 100 million copies are printed each year. It is a book that has truly changed our world.

BIBLE TRANSLATIONS

Are there dangers in some of the
new versions of the Bible?

"Your word I have hidden in my heart, that I might not sin against You" (Psalm 119:11).

First, we need to understand that unless you are looking at the original Hebrew and Greek texts, all Bibles are translations. The question we need to ask is about the quality of a translation and the text sources used. Some translations are really "paraphrases," which means they don't follow the source text closely, but rather loosely and subjectively give the meaning of phrases. Examples of this are the Living Bible or The Message. It is misleading, for example, when the Living Bible calls the mark of the beast a tattoo.

The careful Bible student will recognize that there are some biases in some of the new English translations. For instance, Hebrews 9:12 in some Bibles speaks of the holy place, but in others it speaks of the most holy place. This variation is shaped by different theological viewpoints. That's why it is good to look at several translations that more closely follow the source text word by word, such as the King James, the New King James, and the New American Standard versions.

Sometimes the creation of these new translations is driven by money. Let me explain. The King James Bible is public domain. So in order for publishers to make money selling a Bible, they're required to say something different than existing versions in order to copyright, market, and own it. For instance, you can be sued for copying and quoting the New International Version without permission, because the publishers own that version. They have a monetary motivation to come up with something different, but how many ways can you say the same thing in English?

I personally believe the Lord can work through any version. People have come to Christ in many parts of the world reading many different translations. But if you are doing a deep study on a passage, compare several versions with each other. In church, I like my members to read Scripture out loud from the same translation; otherwise, we start sounding like a barnyard full of confusion! My favorite translations are the King James and the New King James.

PROPHECY TIMELINE

Where are we in the timeline of the prophecies of Revelation?

"Here is the patience of the saints; here are those who keep the commandments of God and the faith of Jesus" (Revelation 14:12).

I believe we are living in the time described in Revelation 13 and 14. These chapters deal with the two great beasts. In chapter 13 the first beast—the one that rises from the sea and has seven heads and ten horns—was wounded, but its "deadly wound was healed." This is a segment of time that has already passed. Then the second beast—which has two horns like a lamb and speaks like a dragon (Revelation 13:11)—comes on the scene and is ready to make an image to the first beast that was healed. It tries to force everyone on Earth to worship the first beast.

According to Daniel 7, these beasts are nations. I believe the second beast is the United States, which accurately fits the description and historical setting. It looks like a lamb; it starts out as a nation founded on Christian principles, but it begins to speak like a dragon.

In prophecy, a lamb is a symbol of Christ and a dragon is a symbol of Satan. We are going to see America bringing the Protestant, Catholic, and Orthodox churches to apostatize—to abandon their distinctive beliefs and come together to form a one-world church that undermines God's law. However, there will be a biblical element who will remain true to God and refuse to receive the mark of the beast, "those who keep the commandments of God and the faith of Jesus" (Revelation 14:12).

I believe we are on the verge of religious laws that will hedge in God's people and force a decision for or against God's moral law. This conflict will spotlight the fourth commandment, the law that focuses on God as Creator. That's why the first angel's message warns us to "worship Him who made heaven and earth, the sea and springs of water" (Revelation 14:7). Those who choose to keep God's law will triumph. Jesus assures us that "he who endures to the end will be saved" (Matthew 10:22).

THE ANTICHRIST

Is the antichrist a person or something else?

"I was considering the horns, and there was another horn, a little one, coming up among them, before whom three of the first horns were plucked out by the roots. And there, in this horn, were eyes like the eyes of a man, and a mouth speaking pompous words" (Daniel 7:8).

We sometimes get sidetracked by identifying *who* the Antichrist is and not focusing on *what* it represents—a corrupt religious power that attempts to take the place of Christ. Certainly there are passages that speak of him having "eyes like the eyes of a man, and a mouth speaking pompous words." The apostle John wrote of this power as having "the number of a man" (Revelation 13:18). Just as Greece was represented by a goat in Daniel 8, with a horn that stood for Alexander the Great, so there will be a figure-leader who is directed by Satan.

But we can be misled when we try to lock on to a specific person, forgetting that it is their *position* that is against God. It is not so much that this religious leader is evil in and of himself. In fact, his rulership has changed hands many times over the centuries. Neither can we assume that all the members of this false religious church are bad, for God has said, "Come out of her, my people" (Revelation 18:4), which means there are still followers of the Lord within this organization.

The system is called "antichrist" because it has usurped Jesus' authority and attempted to change His laws. It also teaches that priests can forgive sins, which only God can do (Luke 5:21); it has attempted to change the commandments by dropping the second one (on worshiping images) and splitting the tenth into two parts. But the Bible says God's law cannot be changed (Matthew 5:18).

It was Satan's original plan in heaven to take God's authority. When he was cast out, he continued to discredit God and use other agencies to try to take over His position. In the final days of history, Satan will use this religious power to unite world governments in a final attempt to control the world and destroy God's people.

Near Death Visions

Does God speak to people through near-death experiences?

"To the law and to the testimony! If they do not speak according to this word, it is because there is no light in them" (Isaiah 8:20).

A number of people claim to have had so-called "near-death experiences" (NDEs), where they died (or almost died) and then came back to share experiences of seeing lights and sometimes meeting angels, Jesus, and even dead relatives. Others speak of "out-of-body" experiences. If you are not familiar with the Bible's teaching on the state of the dead, NDEs can be a very deceptive tool of the devil.

The most important thing to remember is that you should never build your understanding of Scripture based on your senses. Always base it on the Word of God.

A doctor once explained to me what can happen during extreme heart trauma, when the brain is robbed of oxygen. It's very dangerous when you don't get enough oxygen—you can hallucinate and have visions. It's a well-known biological occurrence. A person who claims to have risen out of their body or had a dream during near-death moments might have simply experienced a physiological phenomenon resulting from this lack of oxygen. What they experience might seem real, but it is merely a fantasy of their imagination.

I wouldn't totally rule out the possibility of God speaking to a person through a vision. We have examples of this in the Bible. But I would warn you again that we should never build our theology on near-death experiences. If you ever think the Lord is speaking to you through such a phenomena or even a dream, compare it with the Word of God. Too often the messages people hear are not biblically sound.

Satan will use any means to lead people astray from the Bible. The closer we come to the coming of Christ, the more deceptive will be his practices. Notice Paul's warning: "For such are false apostles, deceitful workers, transforming themselves into apostles of Christ. And no wonder! For Satan himself transforms himself into an angel of light" (2 Corinthians 11:13, 14). We can't always count on our senses for finding truth.

PROPHECY'S BEASTS

In prophecy, does the symbol "beast" mean "beastly" characteristics?

"After this I saw ... a fourth beast, dreadful and terrible, exceedingly strong. It had huge iron teeth; it was devouring, breaking in pieces, and trampling the residue with its feet. It was different from all the beasts that were before it, and it had ten horns" (Daniel 7:7).

D aniel has a strange vision of four beasts coming out of the sea. Like the book of Revelation, Daniel is an "apocalyptic" volume about the last days. These dreams are filled with symbolism. The Bible explains these pictures, often within the very context of the same book. For instance, Daniel 2 is a parallel vision to Daniel 7 and identifies the first kingdom as Babylon (Daniel 2:38, 39). Daniel 8 is also a parallel vision and identifies the second power as Medo-Persia (Daniel 8:20).

The most terrible beast of Daniel 7 is a fourth world kingdom represented by a frightening monster with ten horns and iron teeth. Once more, we find a parallel in Daniel 2, where the fourth kingdom was represented by iron and later divided into 10 nations represented by 10 toes. We know from history that the 10 horns represent 10 kingdoms into which modern-day Europe was divided.

If we define "beastly" as lacking intelligence, we would be fooled, for it has always been Satan's ploy to deceive. In the end, the devil will not raise up some off-the-wall pagan system of religion to lead people astray. His greatest deception is to build a false religion within Christianity itself, a power that looks like the real thing. On the other hand, this false religious power has definitely exhibited brutal characteristics over the centuries in persecuting God's faithful people.

Just before Christ comes, two powers will unite to carry out Satan's final effort to annihilate the Lord's children. They are described in Revelation 13 as the "beast of the sea" that influences the "beast of the earth" to "cause as many as would not worship the image of the beast to be killed" (Revelation 13:14, 15). This beast is powerful and deadly.

THREE ANGELS' MESSAGES

Is it possible to preach Jesus' end-time truth
without including the three angels' messages?

*"The Revelation of Jesus Christ, which God gave Him to show
His servants—things which must shortly take place. And
He sent and signified it by His angel to His servant John"
(Revelation 1:1).*

The book of Revelation is built on a promise: "Blessed is he
who reads and those who hear the words of this prophecy,
and keep those things which are written in it; for the time is
near" (Revelation 1:3). The messages within this sacred book were
not intended to be locked away or ignored. They are to be spread
throughout the world. This is reinforced once more at the end of the
book: "Behold, I am coming quickly! Blessed is he who keeps the
words of the prophecy of this book" (22:7).

Pastors who are faithful to the Word of God will not neglect
preaching on the prophecies found in John's apocalypse. This includes
the special messages of Revelation 14:6–13. Notice that the message of
the first angel is called the "everlasting" gospel. It is not a temporary
sermon for just a few people. It is to go to "every nation, tribe, tongue,
and people" (v. 6).

The message of the second angel states, "Babylon is fallen" (v. 8)
and warns people to come out of Babylon (vv. 1, 2, 4). Unless you
understand that Babylon is a false religious system, you cannot leave
her. This is a message of preparation for the soon coming of Christ.
The third angel's message warns against worshiping "the beast and his
image" (14:9–11). It is a sobering warning that there will soon come a
time when a false religious power will seek to force everyone to break
God's fourth commandment.

These three angels' messages are summed up by identifying God's
people: "Here is the patience of the saints; here are those who keep the
commandments of God and the faith of Jesus" (v. 12). In the face of the
overwhelming deception and persecution that is soon to come, how
could any genuine religious leader not want to warn people?

Secret Societies

Does the Bible say anything about being involved in secret societies?

"No longer do I call you servants, for a servant does not know what his master is doing; but I have called you friends, for all things that I heard from My Father I have made known to you" (John 15:15).

A secret society is a group that often meets in secret places closed to public viewing. Examples include elite organizations, like the Mason society, and even some religions. Throughout the Bible, Jesus says we should walk in the light. When people are doing things in a dark place, it can cast doubt. But Christians should be transparent and shouldn't take secret oaths. Jesus says to let our nays be nays and our yeas be yeas—we shouldn't be swearing by things shrouded in secret. Many policies and principles in secret societies contradict the openness of Christianity.

In John 15:15, Jesus says, "No longer do I call you servants, for a servant does not know what his master is doing; but I have called you friends, for all things that I heard from My Father I have made known to you." Jesus is not keeping secrets; He is being open with us. Honesty, transparency, openness—whatever you want to call it—should be a Christian characteristic.

Another point worth mentioning is that many times, secret societies require members to pledge their allegiance to someone or something other than God. But our full allegiance belongs only to God. He must have first place in our hearts. Jesus said even if we love our own families more than Him, we're not worthy of Him (see Matthew 10:37).

In addition, people who join secret societies are often sworn to obey rules that are in conflict with Scripture. Some have rituals steeped in paganism. They might even pretend to be religious, while members are led to believe they can earn their way to heaven through works, rather than through simple faith in Christ. This kind of teaching contradicts and undermines the gospel. So there are many problems with secret societies, and Christians should definitely steer away from them.

WEDDING RINGS

Is it permissible for Christians to wear wedding rings?

"In like manner also, that the women adorn themselves in modest apparel, with propriety and moderation, not with braided hair or gold or pearls or costly clothing" (1 Timothy 2:9).

Would it surprise you to know that 150 years ago, most Protestants Christians did not wear any jewelry at all, including wedding rings? This symbol reportedly goes back to ancient Babylon, and perhaps even before this time, when a woman was bought as a slave. If she wasn't a virgin, they would put a ring on her finger. Eventually, this practice made its way into Pagan Rome.

Obviously, multitudes of sincere Christians who wore wedding bands will be in heaven, but there is nothing in the Bible that supports the idea of wearing the symbol as a marker of marriage. You might hear all sorts of euphoric sermons on how it represents the "eternal circle of love," but it's all concocted by men.

Once Christians compromise with human traditions and make concessions to wear jewelry, there is no real end to it. What I have found as a pastor is that once a little hole in the dam appears, the dam will eventually break. Today, professed Christians are piercing and hanging multiple minerals all over their bodies. I don't believe God wants us to do that; it's just another custom to get you to buy stuff you don't really need.

Because we wrestle with sin and temptation, now is not the time to glorify our exteriors. The supreme goal of the Christian is to attract attention to Christ, not to self. Decorating our mortal bodies with glittering gems usually springs from pride, which is diametrically opposed to the spirit and principles of Jesus. "Whoever exalts himself will be humbled, and he who humbles himself will be exalted" (Matthew 23:12).

The wearing of the wedding ring has become a widely accepted tradition. But if sincere seekers of God study this topic and are convicted to remove all jewelry from their body temples, God will give them the grace to follow Him above man's popular tradition. "All too well you reject the commandment of God, that you may keep your tradition" (Mark 7:9).

FOOD AND SALVATION

Will people who eat unclean animals—such as
pork, shrimp, lobster, etc.—go to heaven?

*"Truly, these times of ignorance God overlooked, but now
commands all men everywhere to repent" (Acts 17:30).*

This question addresses people who eat the animals that God
calls unclean and are unfit for human consumption. Is it a sin?
Well, it depends on what the Lord has revealed to the person.
The Bible shows that if we know that God forbids eating these things,
we should avoid eating them.

For instance, in Daniel 1, the Babylonians offered the prophet
Daniel a diet that included unclean foods. He said, "I cannot defile
myself with a portion of the king's food." He would rather have died
before he ate the Babylonian food because he knew better. It's really
a question of loyalty; what will you do when you learn the truth? For
certain, there will most likely be an uncountable number of believers
in the kingdom who probably ate things that the Bible calls forbidden,
simply because they didn't know any better. This is why Acts 17:30
says, "These times of ignorance God overlooked." When we don't have
the knowledge, God shows us mercy.

Sin is defined as knowing good but not doing it; that's one of the
Bible definitions: "Therefore, to him who knows to do good and does
not do it, to him it is sin" (James 4:17). When we know God's will and
don't do what He asks, that's a sin.

First Corinthians 3:16 asks us, "Do you not know that you are
the temple of God and that the Spirit of God dwells in you?" This
makes it perfectly clear that our body is God's temple. It matters to the
Lord how we treat that temple. So whether it's keeping the Sabbath or
honoring our body as a temple of the Holy Spirit, God wants us to live
up to the light He gives us. If you know the truth but don't act on it,
what does that tell God?

WORD OF GOD INSPIRED

Is all of the Bible inspired or only parts of it?

"All Scripture is given by inspiration of God, and is profitable for doctrine, for reproof, for correction, for instruction in righteousness" (2 Timothy 3:16).

The testimony of the Bible's inspiration is found in 2 Timothy 3:16, which clearly states *all* Scripture is inspired of God. When we are tempted to take out a pair of scissors and cut out those passages that we don't like or think are not inspired, we place ourselves above Scripture. We put ourselves in a position to judge the Word of God, rather than letting the Bible be our judge.

Some believe there are "degrees of inspiration" in the Bible. They feel some stories are exaggerated, some histories are glorified, and some narratives are symbolic even though they might not be presented that way. Modern skeptics reject the story of Adam and Eve, question the worldwide flood, and doubt that a fish swallowed a man and then later spewed him out on a beach.

Yet Scripture itself provides no variation in its contents. What makes the Bible's content accurate? How is it that all of its historical narratives are true? The answer is divine inspiration. I accept all of Scripture as divinely inspired; even the parts that are hard for me to understand reveal God's plan to save people. I am continually awed that even within the shadows of Old Testament stories that seem useless, I suddenly find pictures of Jesus. Through faithful and persistent study, I have found hidden truths of gold.

It's no limitation on the part of the Bible that I don't see these inspired teachings; it's because of my own lack of faith. We need to be more like the blind man to whom Jesus asked, "What do you want Me to do for you?" (Mark 10:51). Like this man who could not see, we need to pray, "Rabboni, that I may receive my sight," and then hear Jesus reply, "Go your way; your faith has made you well." Mark then writes, "And immediately he received his sight and followed Jesus on the road" (v. 52).

UNDERSTANDING GOD'S WORD

If the Bible is truly God's book, shouldn't everyone be able to understand it?

"These things we also speak, not in words which man's wisdom teaches but which the Holy Spirit teaches, comparing spiritual things with spiritual. But the natural man does not receive the things of the Spirit of God, for they are foolishness to him; nor can he know them, because they are spiritually discerned" (1 Corinthians 2:13, 14).

Have you ever tried to watch a movie in 3-D *without* those funny-looking glasses? It looks blurry, right? (You might even get a headache doing it.) Though the industry is working to make these lenses unnecessary, most 3-D films are shown from two projectors perfectly lined up and displaying two images on the same screen. The polarization of those special glasses corrects the fuzzy picture and separates the images, making them clear.

Likewise, some people see only blurry images when they read the Bible. It just doesn't make sense to them. They wonder, "What is the point of that strange service in which animals are sacrificed in the Old Testament?" And the death of Jesus on the cross appears to be a waste of someone's life. I believe the Bible doesn't seem clear to some people because there's a missing element: Like special glasses, we need to put on the lenses of faith.

Bright people who can understand and explain virtually anything else are often quickly stopped in their tracks when they read the Bible. The reason is that spiritual things "are spiritually discerned" (1 Corinthians 2:14). The deep things of the Word will never be understood by a secular mind, no matter how brilliant. Unless one honestly seeks an experience with God, he cannot understand the things of God. The Holy Spirit, who explains the Bible, is not understood by the carnal mind. On the other hand, the humble, even uneducated Christian who studies the Bible receives amazing understanding from the Holy Spirit.

So put on faith when you read the Bible. Sincerely pray for the Holy Spirit to open your eyes to discern truth. And be prepared to have your vision expanded!

BIBLE ERRORS

How can anyone believe the Bible is inspired when it's full of errors?

"The words of the LORD are pure words, like silver tried in a furnace of earth, purified seven times" (Psalm 12:6).

First, the overwhelming majority of so-called errors in the Bible have been demonstrated to be a lack of understanding on the part of those who make this complaint. They are not errors at all, but simply truth misunderstood. The Bible will always tell you the truth, will never mislead you, and is reliable and authoritative, not only in spiritual matters but also in history and science.

Archaeologists have uncovered more than 25,000 sites that confirm the reliable history found in the Bible. There are over 2,000 fulfilled biblical prophecies, some with great detail, such as what we read in Isaiah 53 about the Messiah. And New Testament eyewitnesses to events are numerous. Most writers either personally saw Jesus or interviewed an eyewitness close to Him.

Some ask, "Were not errors made in copying manuscripts down through the centuries?" It's true that minor copy errors were made in some manuscripts. Almost all of them are easily explained as simple mistakes in copying. But what is most impressive about this is that only one-fifth of one percent are worth considering, and even these do not affect the clear doctrines of the Bible. It's interesting that compared to the best copied work in antiquity, the *Iliad*, which is also considered a "sacred" work by some, the New Testament is 25 times more accurate. Even more amazing is that while the *Iliad* has 643 ancient copies available, the New Testament has more than 24,000!

Satan is always digging up some supposed flaw in Scripture, which is not surprising. He found fault even with God and heaven. Copyists might have miscopied in some cases, but no such supposed happening or any other alleged error affects the truth of God's Word. Doctrine is built not upon one Bible passage, but upon the total of God's comments on any subject. There will always be room for doubt to those who prefer to doubt. Yet the harder people work to undermine the Bible, the brighter its light shines.

Jesus' Body

What kind of body does Jesus have right now—physical or spirit?

"Jesus came and stood in the midst, and said to them, 'Peace be with you.' When He had said this, He showed them His hands and His side" (John 20:19, 20).

There is more than one description of Jesus after the resurrection showing that He was not just a spirit floating around; He had a body of flesh and bone. Notice this post-resurrection appearance to the disciples:

"Now as they said these things, Jesus Himself stood in the midst of them, and said to them, 'Peace to you.' But they were terrified and frightened, and supposed they had seen a spirit. And He said to them, 'Why are you troubled? And why do doubts arise in your hearts? Behold My hands and My feet, that it is I Myself. Handle Me and see, for a spirit does not have flesh and bones as you see I have.' When He had said this, He showed them His hands and His feet. But while they still did not believe for joy, and marveled, He said to them, 'Have you any food here?' So they gave Him a piece of a broiled fish and some honeycomb. And He took it and ate in their presence" (Luke 24:36–43).

There are lots of details that show Christ had a body—mind you, a resurrected body that was incorruptible and not tainted with sin. The disciple Mary touched this real body after the resurrection (John 20:17). Jesus invited Thomas to physically touch His hands, feet, and side (John 20:27). Christ met the disciples for breakfast by the Sea of Tiberias (John 21:1–14).

Finally, Christ walked with His disciples out to Bethany, where He lifted up His hands and blessed them before ascending into heaven (Luke 24:50). Notice what the two angels say to the disciples: "This same Jesus, who was taken up from you into heaven, will so come in like manner as you saw Him go into heaven" (Acts 1:11). Just as they saw Jesus with a physical body then, we will likewise see Him when He comes back the second time.

THE NATURE OF SATAN

Does the Bible portray the devil as a red, beast-like creature with horns?

"Satan himself transforms himself into an angel of light" (2 Corinthians 11:14).

We've all seen those pictures of Satan dressed in red carrying a three-pronged spear used to torment sinners in hell. But you'll never find this depiction in the Bible. Before his fall, Satan's name was Lucifer, and he was described in glowing terms. The Bible speaks of him with the "seal of perfection, full of wisdom and perfect in beauty" (Ezekiel 28:12). But all of that changed when he tried to stand in the place of God. He was "cast as a profane thing out of the mountain of God" (v. 16).

The portrayal of the devil as a monster with horns and a pitchfork crept into the church during the Middle Ages, when Christian leaders combined pagan religions with Bible teachings. It not only corrupted many doctrines, it also brought in a mixture of pagan deities that were modified to connect with characters in Scripture. In the ancient Greek religion, one mythological figure was the demigod Pan, who is shown with the hindquarters, legs, and horns of a goat.

Artists during this period made paintings and sculptures showing the devil in these grotesque ways, sometimes with chicken legs, or covered in animal hair, or with scars and boils and other deformities. Combined with these twisted pictures is the unbiblical view that the devil is now in hell. The Bible says he "walks about like a roaring lion, seeking whom he may devour" (1 Peter 5:8). Satan is not trapped in hell but roams the earth to deceive and destroy (Job 1:7).

I think the devil is delighted to have himself pictured as a strange mythological figure. He knows that thinking people will reject monsters and fables, and so they deny his existence. But those who do not believe he exists are most likely to be captured by his wiles. The Scriptures teach that Satan deceives (Revelation 12:9), works miracles (John 8:44), misquotes the Bible (Matthew 4:5, 6), and even calls fire from heaven (Revelation 13:13). The devil is real, and we should not be deceived by his lies.

THE WICKED

Will the wicked be able to see the righteous who are inside the New Jerusalem?

"Wait on the LORD, and keep His way, and He shall exalt you to inherit the land; when the wicked are cut off, you shall see it" (Psalm 37:34).

Someone once asked Jesus, "Are there few who are saved?" (Luke 13:23). Christ encouraged people to strive to be in His kingdom, and then warned, "There will be weeping and gnashing of teeth, when you see Abraham and Isaac and Jacob and all the prophets in the kingdom of God, and yourselves thrust out" (v. 28). This verse, along with Psalm 37:34, seems to indicate that the wicked will see the righteous and the righteous will see the wicked before the final destruction of sin and sinners.

You might wonder how people inside a walled city could see out or those on the outside could see in. John gives us a clue when he describes the Holy City as it comes down out of heaven to this earth: "Her light was like a most precious stone, like a jasper stone, clear as crystal" (Revelation 21:11). And also, "The construction of its wall was of jasper; and the city was pure gold, like clear glass" (v. 18). It's hard to imagine something so beautiful and transparent!

At the end of the millennium, the Bible tells us Satan will be released to deceive the nations one last time. As he gathers people from all over the earth, it says, "They went up on the breadth of the earth and surrounded the camp of the saints and the beloved city" (Revelation 20:9). We don't exactly know how long these events will take, but verse three tells us the devil is released for "a little while."

This does mean there could be some very sad encounters at the walls of the New Jerusalem before fire comes down to destroy the wicked. Perhaps the saved could look through the walls and see outside the sad faces of lost family and friends on the other side looking back at them. Such possible heartache should move us to work and pray earnestly for all those we love to be inside the kingdom, including ourselves.

THE SACRIFICIAL SYSTEM

Why did animals need to be sacrificed in the Old Testament sanctuary services?

"According to the law almost all things are purified with blood, and without shedding of blood there is no remission" (Hebrews 9:22).

The sacrificing of animals was necessary to help people understand that without the shedding of Jesus' blood, their sins could never be forgiven. The ugly, shocking truth is that the punishment for sin is eternal death. Since all of us have sinned, all of us should die. When Adam and Eve sinned, they would have died at once except for Jesus, who stepped forward and offered to give His perfect life as a sacrifice to pay the death penalty for all people.

After sin, God required the sinner to bring an animal sacrifice (Genesis 4:3–7). When a sinner brought a sacrificial animal to the door of the courtyard, a priest handed him a knife and a basin. The sinner laid his hands on the animal's head and confessed his sins. This symbolized the transfer of sin from the sinner to the animal. At that point, the sinner was considered innocent and the animal guilty. Since the animal was now symbolically guilty, it had to pay sin's wage—death.

The sinner was to kill the animal with his own hand (Leviticus 1:4, 5). It was bloody and shocking. By slaying the animal, the sinner was graphically taught that sin caused the innocent animal's death and that his sin would cause the death of the innocent Jesus. It indelibly impressed the sinner with the solemn reality of sin's awful consequences (eternal death) and the desperate need of a Savior.

The sacrificial system taught, through the symbol of the slain animal, that God would give His Son to die for their sins (1 Corinthians 15:3). Jesus would become not only their Savior, but also their substitute (Hebrews 9:28). When John the Baptist met Jesus, he said, "Behold! The Lamb of God who takes away the sin of the world!" (John 1:29). In the Old Testament, people looked forward to the cross for salvation. We look backward to Calvary for salvation. There is no other source of salvation.

The Lost

How will the destruction of wicked angels and people affect God?

"'As I live,' says the Lord God, 'I have no pleasure in the death of the wicked, but that the wicked turn from his way and live. Turn, turn from your evil ways! For why should you die, O house of Israel?'" (Ezekiel 33:11).

Sometimes we try to place on God the attributes of sinful human beings. We think that the Lord somehow feels like we do about wicked people, especially those who have deeply hurt us or our family and friends. But God is not like us. The Lord says, "For My thoughts are not your thoughts, nor are your ways My ways" (Isaiah 55:8). This is true when it comes to the punishment of evil.

While it is accurate to say that God will punish sinful people who do not turn from their ways, destroying them in the lake of fire where they will be totally consumed, it is not done with delight. Listen to God's heart in Scripture. Ezekiel presents the emotions of a Father who cries for His children.

I am touched by these words depicting this longing for the lost: "How can I give you up, Ephraim? How can I hand you over, Israel?...My heart churns within Me; My sympathy is stirred" (Hosea 11:8). Any normal parent can sense the terrible pain in God's heart when He looks at His wayward children.

Sadly, even Jesus' disciples didn't sense that the teacher they came to love was similar in character to God the Father. Notice how Christ presented the Father: "In that day you will ask in My name, and I do not say to you that I shall pray the Father for you; *for the Father Himself loves you*, because you have loved Me, and have believed that I came forth from God" (John 16:26, 27, my emphasis).

All of our heavenly family will grieve over the destruction of those who refuse to receive the gift of eternal life. It should motivate us now to reach out to them before it is too late.

HEALTH LAWS

Are health laws in the Bible really that important—isn't it enough to just love God?

"Having been perfected, He became the author of eternal salvation to all who obey Him" (Hebrews 5:9).

Imagine with me for a moment a man who courts a woman for a couple years. He sends her letters and flowers. He takes her on dates and spends lots of time communicating his heart to her. He listens and cares about her needs. This man goes out of his way to be attentive because he is in love.

But what would happen if he sat around and watched TV all day after they get married? What if he never tried to get a job, never assisted around the house, never took her on dates, and never listened to her heart? What would you think if you confronted him and he replied, "I love my wife; isn't that enough?" My response would be, "What kind of love is that?"

Salvation can never be earned by obedience, but obedience is the result of exercising faith in Christ. When we truly love Jesus, we will want to obey Him (John 14:15). It will be the natural bent of our heart. We will see God's laws of health not as restrictions to take away our fun, but as guidelines that protect us and lead us into a happier life.

Obedience to God's health laws goes hand in hand with faith. Some people think their faith means these laws are meaningless. But the Bible says, "Do we then make void the law through faith? Certainly not! On the contrary, we establish the law" (Romans 3:31). My faith in Jesus will lead me to ask, "How can I show my love for a Savior who gave His life for me?"

Following all sorts of health laws out of a legalistic obligation driven by an effort to "earn" salvation will never work. It is a focus based on ourselves and not on Christ. But genuine faith that accepts God's free offer of salvation will transform our hearts and lead us to care for our bodies because it is through our minds that we study the Bible and listen to the Holy Spirit speak to our hearts.

Mistakenly Saved?

Is it really possible for someone to be lost who truly thinks he is saved?

"Not everyone who says to Me, 'Lord, Lord,' shall enter the kingdom of heaven, but he who does the will of My Father in heaven" (Matthew 7:21).

Have you ever been driving down the freeway on a beautiful day and enjoying yourself when suddenly you notice flashing red and blue lights behind you? Your first thought might be, "Oh no! Was I speeding?" You glance down and, sure enough, you're going 15 miles an hour over the speed limit. What would the highway patrol officer say to you if you told him, "But I didn't *mean* to speed!" or "I *thought* I was going the speed limit!"

The fact is—you still broke the law.

Likewise, Jesus warns us that some people might *think* they are going down the road to heaven, enjoying themselves, and minding their own business. But what they think does not change God's expectations. Christ said you can know that you are on the path to eternal life if you are seeking to do "the will of My Father in heaven." Truth is not shaped by our feelings or hopes. It stands solid, regardless of what *we* might think. So how do we know we are doing God's will?

We know we are going in the right direction when there is an intimate connection between ourselves and the Lord. It's more than just doing the "right" things. "Many will say to Me in that day, 'Lord, Lord, have we not prophesied in Your name, cast out demons in Your name, and done many wonders in Your name?'" (Matthew 7:22). These are all good things, but there is something more that goes deeper than outward actions.

Jesus explains to outward doers of the law, "I never knew you; depart from Me, you who practice lawlessness!" (v. 23). When we try to carry out God's law without a changed heart, the actions are worthless. It shows that we are not really doing God's will because our motives have not changed. People who have the assurance of salvation live lives of service motivated by unselfish love. This is the will of the Father in heaven.

GOD'S WORD

Why does the Bible share repugnant and graphic descriptions of sin? Is it really necessary?

"For whatever things were written before were written for our learning, that we through the patience and comfort of the Scriptures might have hope" (Romans 15:4).

The fact that the Bible openly shares the sins of different people is one reason it has such credibility. Archaeologists have discovered many histories of kings and kingdoms; most of their battle scenes and depictions of royalty are exaggerated and leave out the defects of main characters, which the Bible does not do.

Even today, biographies skip over or soften the bad and overstate the good. So "telling it like it is" gives people more confidence that the Bible can be trusted. It doesn't cover up everything or give a glorified picture of Israel or Jesus' disciples.

The winner of a war often gets to chronicle the story, and it's often more glorification and propaganda than fact. There are hundreds of examples of efforts to cover up the facts regarding nations that have committed war crimes—even retouching photos to hide the truth. The Bible does not gloss over the sins of even its greatest leaders, such as King David, who not only committed adultery, an acceptable practice of most kings in those days, but also murder to cover up his trail.

Satan wants to convince people that we are such terrible sinners that God could never save us. Yet time and again, the Lord redeems His people. When Israel turned away from the Lord, the nation was exiled into Babylon. Yet God heard their cries and said, "But now, thus says the LORD, who created you, O Jacob, and He who formed you, O Israel: 'Fear not, for I have redeemed you; I have called you by your name; you are Mine'" (Isaiah 43:1).

We can learn from David, who repented and was forgiven by God. We can have hope when we read of how Peter denied Christ, but bitterly wept and was restored. Such stories strengthen our faith.

ASKING FOR SIGNS

Is it safe to ask God for a sign that He wants me to obey?

"An evil and adulterous generation seeks after a sign, and no sign will be given to it except the sign of the prophet Jonah" (Matthew 12:39).

There are some examples in the Bible in which people have asked the Lord for a sign and God responded to their request. Gideon was an Old Testament soldier called by God to lead an army and save Israel from the Midianites. He humbly asked for more than one sign, to which the Angel of the Lord obliged (see Judges 6:11–40).

But in the New Testament, we find a sobering statement by Christ to the scribes and Pharisees who said, "Teacher, we want to see a sign from You" (Matthew 12:38). You might think this is an innocent request, but if you look at the whole chapter, you see constant opposition against Jesus. They accuse Him of breaking the Sabbath, they plot to destroy Him, and claim He uses the power of Satan.

It is to these wicked leaders that Christ said, "An evil and adulterous generation seeks after a sign." Jesus had plainly spoken to them. Evidence of His divine mission had already been shown, yet they continued to resist Him. Unlike Gideon, their motives were not genuine. They were not seeking to believe, but to destroy. A sign would not change their hearts. They were not interested in God's truth.

Christ once said of these stubborn religious leaders, "If they do not hear Moses and the prophets, neither will they be persuaded though one rise from the dead" (Luke 16:31). Notice their response to Lazarus being raised from the dead. "Then the chief priests and the Pharisees gathered a council and said, 'What shall we do? For this Man works many signs.' … Then, from that day on, they plotted to put Him to death" (John 11:47, 53).

When the Word of God has been plainly spoken, we do not need a sign to determine whether we should obey the Lord. If our motive is to follow God, He will make the truth plain to us.

THE TRANSFIGURATION

Did Moses and Elijah actually appear with Jesus at the transfiguration, or was it only a vision?

"Behold, Moses and Elijah appeared to them, talking with Him" (Matthew 17:3).

After Peter, James, and John saw the transfiguration, Matthew writes, "As they came down from the mountain, Jesus commanded them, saying, 'Tell the vision to no one until the Son of Man is risen from the dead'" (Matthew 17:9). Some people have wondered what is meant by the word "vision." Did they really see Jesus with Moses and Elijah, or was it simply a dream?

We have reasons to believe this was a literal event. First, Matthew says that Moses and Elijah "appeared" to them and spoke with Christ. Second, we can find in the Bible that these two prophets are not sleeping in their graves, but are alive in heaven. Jude 9, for instance, speaks of a dispute over the body of Moses, which could only mean Satan wanted to prevent Christ from resurrecting him from the dead. And 2 Kings 2:1, 11, and 12, clearly show us that Elijah did not taste death but was taken up into heaven in a chariot of fire.

It's helpful to remember that English words have been translated from the Greek (in the New Testament) and that the word "horama" rendered as "vision" in verse 9, can also mean "spectacle" or, literally, "that which is seen." In other words, Jesus was saying, "Tell no one what you saw." It was wise counsel, since it would have only raised curiosities and not served a good purpose as much as it did after Christ's resurrection.

Moses and Elijah were religious leaders who suffered terrible onslaughts from the devil and from God's own people. They understood what Jesus was passing through and came to encourage Him and remind Him of all who would be brought into the kingdom. Some, like Moses, would experience death but be resurrected. Others, when Christ comes, will be like Elijah and not taste death. These two men were the perfect representatives of heaven to give support to Jesus, who was about to face the greatest tribulation of anyone through all time.

SINCERITY AND ZEAL

When it comes to salvation, are sincerity and zeal enough?

"[God] has saved us and called us with a holy calling, not according to our works, but according to His own purpose and grace which was given to us in Christ Jesus before time began" *(2 Timothy 1:9).*

One of the sincerest religious people in the Bible was Saul of Tarsus. He explained his credentials by stating, "I am indeed a Jew, born in Tarsus of Cilicia, but brought up in this city at the feet of Gamaliel, taught according to the strictness of our fathers' law, and was zealous toward God as you all are today" (Acts 22:3).

But his fervor took a sudden turn: "I persecuted this Way to the death, binding and delivering into prison both men and women, as also the high priest bears me … from whom I also received letters to the brethren, and went to Damascus to bring in chains even those who were there to Jerusalem to be punished" (vv. 4, 5).

When it came to salvation, the man who would become the apostle Paul didn't need more zeal. He needed a converted heart. We can sincerely try to do what we think is right, but it might be very wrong. That's why we must come before the Searcher of all hearts; we must expose ourselves to Bible truth and ask God to convict us of sin. Unless we repent and turn from self, our best efforts to do right are like filthy rags (Isaiah 64:6). The most respected religious teacher in Israel, Nicodemus, was told quite directly by Christ that he needed to be "born again" (John 3:3).

Zeal and sincerity are not bad in and of themselves, but in an unconverted heart they can lead us astray, like in the life of Saul. If we were to replace the word zeal for "my best efforts" and then ask, "Will not my best efforts save me?" the Bible answer is "No!" Even good works will not save us. "Not by works of righteousness which we have done, but according to His mercy He saved us, through the washing of regeneration and renewing of the Holy Spirit" (Titus 3:5).

UNITED THEOCRACY

Doesn't it make good sense for governments to pass laws enforcing Christianity?

"If it seems evil to you to serve the LORD, choose for yourselves this day whom you will serve. ... But as for me and my house, we will serve the LORD" (Joshua 24:15).

One of the great principles of freedom is to worship according to the dictates of one's own conscience. God doesn't force people to accept the gift of salvation or to follow His laws. People can freely turn away if they so choose. Guarding this principle once drove the Protestant theologian Roger Williams out of the original colonies! He insisted that every person should have liberty to worship God according to the light of his own convictions.

The U.S. Constitution explains these rights: "No religious test shall ever be required as a qualification to any office of public trust under the United States." And also, "Congress shall make no law respecting an establishment of religion, or prohibiting the free exercise thereof." The framers of our constitution had only to look back into their history to recognize that some of the cruelest wars and persecutions grew from governments who insisted on passing laws to enforce Christianity.

The Lord knows that people forced to obey laws won't live them out of a heart filled with gratitude and love. The Bible teaches, "God is love" (1 John 4:8), and, "There is no fear in love; but perfect love casts out fear, because fear involves torment. But he who fears has not been made perfect in love" (1 John 4:18). Living out of fear of being punished is not how the government of God functions. The Lord desires us to live out of reason and devotion to Him.

It is the mark of Satan's government to use force to control individual thought. The devil's hand has shaped many despots, kings, and rulers to insist people follow laws that determine when, where, and how they must worship. Those who disobeyed were threatened, tortured, banned, and sometimes murdered— all in the name of Christianity. It should never be the role of earthly governments to regulate how people are to worship God.

WORKING FOR RIGHTEOUSNESS?

Does a person have any role at all to play in becoming righteous by faith?

"Not everyone who says to Me, 'Lord, Lord,' shall enter the kingdom of heaven, but he who does the will of My Father in heaven" (Matthew 7:21).

If you picture that salvation is a matter of simply saying a short prayer and then sitting around like a couch potato, you're missing the point of what it means to be saved from sin. God wants to give us a new heart. This happens through our *cooperation* with divine power. We use our free will to seek to do God's will. This is a daily choice. Even in the Old Testament, God's people continued to bring a lamb to the temple, not just once, but as often as they sinned. We need to exercise an ongoing faith and have a wholehearted desire to let the Lord totally lead in our lives.

We cannot change ourselves. There is no power within us to become righteous. We need help from the outside. We must daily recommit to Jesus and invite Him to control our lives. He is the one who performs the miracle. We earnestly *work with* God by abiding in Jesus. We must be willing to be obedient and to follow where Jesus leads (Isaiah 1:18–20).

Sin causes us to want to have our own way (Isaiah 53:6) and, thus, rebel against the Lord, just as Satan did in the beginning (Isaiah 14:12–14). Permitting Jesus to rule our lives is sometimes as difficult as having an eye plucked out (Matthew 5:29, 30), because sin is addictive and can be overcome only by God's miraculous power (Mark 10:27).

Many believe that Jesus will take all who merely profess salvation to heaven, regardless of their conduct afterward. But according to Matthew 7:21, this is not true. It is a fabrication of Satan. A converted Christian must and will follow Jesus' lifestyle (1 Peter 2:21). The powerful blood of Jesus can accomplish this for all (Hebrews 13:12), but only if we give Jesus full control of our lives and follow where He leads— even though the path might sometimes be rough.

REFUSING TITHE

Is it okay to refuse to pay tithe if I don't agree with what the church is doing with it?

"All the tithe of the land, whether of the seed of the land or of the fruit of the tree, is the LORD's. It is holy to the LORD" *(Leviticus 27:30).*

Tithing is a command of God (Malachi 3:10). Tithe is holy money that belongs to the Lord; you return tithe to Him only. Of course, the Lord is able to care for these gifts to His church, so your first responsibility is to tithe. He has chosen individuals to decide how to use tithe based on His guidelines. If they make a mistake, that shouldn't stop you from fulfilling your responsibility.

The Bible says we are to bring the whole tithe to the storehouse in the community where we live (see Malachi 3:10). Old Testament priests did not live only in Jerusalem (Deuteronomy 14:27). They were scattered throughout Israel (Nehemiah 11:1). Yet tithe was still brought to the Levites as God's ministers, wherever they lived. They in turn brought a tenth of the tithes they received to the temple (Nehemiah 10:37, 38; Numbers 18:25–32).

It's natural for people to want to show honor to their local pastor. But this should not be the motivation for returning tithes. Our desire should spring from our love for God and a commitment to follow Scripture guidelines, regardless of how we feel about our pastor.

It is possible that funds could be misused, but it doesn't excuse us from this Christian responsibility to tithe. The chances of gifts being mishandled are probably low. If a member gives to a ministry that has appropriate financial accountability structures in place, he or she can trust that the gift will go to the right place. If there is a concern, there are appropriate channels for remedy.

It's interesting that Jesus chose to pay a temple tax even though He knew this very organization would condemn Him to die (Matthew 17:24–27). He also honored a widow who gave her last few coins to this same church because she was seeking to honor God (Mark 12:41–44). The possibility of mishandling funds should not deter us from returning our tithes to the Lord.

LORD AND SAVIOR

What is the difference between accepting Jesus as my "Savior" and accepting Him as "Lord"?

"Till we all come to the unity of the faith and of the knowledge of the Son of God, to a perfect man, to the measure of the stature of the fullness of Christ" (Ephesians 4:13).

The difference between accepting Christ as a Savior and as a Lord is substantial. When I accept Him as Savior, He saves me from the guilt and penalty of sin and gives me the new birth. He changes me from sinner to saint. This transaction is a glorious miracle and is essential to salvation. No one can be saved without it. "Therefore, as through one man's offense judgment came to all men, resulting in condemnation, even so through one Man's righteous act the free gift came to all men, resulting in justification of life" (Romans 5:18).

However, Jesus is not finished with me at this point. I have been born again, but His plan is that I also grow up to become more like Him, as Ephesians 4:13 says, into "the stature of the fullness of Christ." When I accept Him daily as the ruler, or Lord, of my life, He, by His miracles, causes me to grow in grace and Christian conduct until I am mature in Christ.

The problem is that I want to run my own life, to have my own way. The Bible calls this mindset "iniquity," or sin (Isaiah 53:6). Making Jesus my Lord is so important that the New Testament mentions Him as "Lord" 766 times. In the book of Acts alone, He is referred to as "Lord" 110 times and as "Savior" only twice. This demonstrates how important it is to know Him as Lord and Ruler of our lives.

Jesus placed continuing emphasis upon His Lordship because He knew that crowning Him Lord would be a forgotten and neglected imperative (2 Corinthians 4:5). Unless I make Him Lord of my life, there is no way I can ever become a full-grown Christian. Instead, I will end up "wretched, miserable, poor, blind, and naked" and, even worse, feeling that I "have need of nothing" (Revelation 3:17).

GOD AND LUCIFER

Since God created Lucifer, isn't He really responsible for sin?

"You were perfect in your ways from the day you were created, till iniquity was found in you" (Ezekiel 28:15).

Not at all. God created Lucifer a perfect, sinless angel. Lucifer made a devil of himself. Freedom to choose is a cornerstone principle of God's government. The Lord knew Lucifer would sin when He created him. If at that point God had refused to create him, He would have been giving up that prime principle of free choice.

So knowing full well what Lucifer would do, God still created him. The same facts apply to the creation of Adam and Eve. And, closer to home, these facts apply to you and me. God knows before we are born how we will live, but even so, He permits us to live and to choose whether to endorse His government or Satan's. God is willing to be misjudged, falsely accused, and blamed for ages, while taking the time to allow every person to freely choose whom he or she will follow.

Only a loving God would risk granting full freedom for all. This glorious, crucial gift of freedom could come only from a just, open, and loving being. It is an honor and joy to serve such a Lord and friend. Freely choosing to follow the Lord leads to greater freedom. "Stand fast therefore in the liberty by which Christ has made us free, and do not be entangled again with a yoke of bondage" (Galatians 5:1). It is God's desire to set us free so that we are no longer "slaves of sin" (Romans 6:6).

The sin problem will soon end. John said, "Now I saw a new heaven and a new earth, for the first heaven and the first earth had passed away" (Revelation 21:1). In the beginning, everything was "very good" (Genesis 1:31). Now "the whole world lies under the sway of the wicked one" (1 John 5:19). Soon Earth will be restored to God's original plan. Until then, people everywhere are choosing to serve God or Satan. Use your fantastic, God-given freedom to choose to serve the Lord.

WINE OF BABYLON

What are the false teachings in the "wine" of Babylon that make people spiritually drunk and confused?

"Yet they did not obey or incline their ear, but everyone followed the dictates of his evil heart" (Jeremiah 11:8).

Amazingly, some of the most prominent doctrines of Protestantism today are not found in the Bible at all. Paganism has been brought in to these churches. A few of these false teachings are:

1. *The law of God has been amended or repealed.* God's law can never be changed or repealed. Jesus said, "It is easier for heaven and earth to pass away than" for the law to fail (Luke 16:17).

2. *The soul is immortal.* The Bible mentions "soul" and "spirit" 1,700 times. Not once is either referred to as immortal. People are mortal (Job 4:17), and none receive immortality until Jesus' second coming. The apostle Paul writes that "we shall all be changed" *when* "this mortal must put on immortality" (1 Corinthians 15:51, 53).

3. *Sinners burn eternally in hell.* The Bible teaches that sinners will be completely consumed (put out of existence), both soul and body, in the fires of hell (Matthew 10:28).

4. *Sunday is God's holy day.* The Bible teaches, without question, that God's holy day is the seventh-day Sabbath, Saturday. "Remember the Sabbath day, to keep it holy. Six days you shall labor and do all your work, but the seventh day is the Sabbath of the LORD your God" (Exodus 20:8–10).

When we accept the false teachings of Babylon, we will become confused, which is what the term "Babylon" literally means. It's sobering to think that some might unknowingly be drinking Babylon's wine. If this is all new to you, ask God to guide you (Matthew 7:7). Search the Scriptures to see if these things are so (Acts 17:11). Follow where Jesus leads, and you will not end up in error.

Devil's Harassment

Why does it seem like I'm being harassed by the devil after joining God's end-time church?

"Therefore rejoice, O heavens, and you who dwell in them! Woe to the inhabitants of the earth and the sea! For the devil has come down to you, having great wrath, because he knows that he has a short time" (Revelation 12:12).

The Bible tells us that our great enemy, the devil, is angry with God's remnant people. His desire is to hurt them, to discourage them, and ultimately to destroy them. Speaking of Satan and the church, the Bible says, "The dragon was enraged with the woman, and he went to make war with the rest of her offspring, who keep the commandments of God and have the testimony of Jesus" (Revelation 12:17).

There are many statements about trials and tribulations in Scripture. The Lord did not promise His people they would be immune to difficulties. "Yes, and all who desire to live godly in Christ Jesus will suffer persecution" (2 Timothy 3:12). King David wrote, "Many are the afflictions of the righteous, but the LORD delivers him out of them all" (Psalm 34:19). God's people in every age have suffered for their faith in Him.

Yet we are not left without hope in the midst of our trials. "Blessed is the man who endures temptation; for when he has been approved, he will receive the crown of life which the Lord has promised to those who love Him" (James 1:12). "These things I have spoken to you, that in Me you may have peace. In the world you will have tribulation; but be of good cheer, I have overcome the world" (John 16:33).

Satan is full of hatred toward the Lord's children. He is bent on trying to turn you away from God. But even though such things will come, the Lord has not left us alone. Like the commander Joshua in leading God's people, the Lord says to you, "I will not leave you nor forsake you" (Joshua 1:5). The tighter we hold onto God's hand during these trials, the safer we will be (John 10:28, 29).

BABYLON AND BABEL

Did Satan's kingdom called "Babylon" originate at the tower of Babel?

"They said, 'Come, let us build ourselves a city, and a tower whose top is in the heavens; let us make a name for ourselves, lest we be scattered abroad over the face of the whole earth" *(Genesis 11:4).*

The tower of Babel spoken of in Genesis 11 was erected by the people of Shinar in opposition to God's instructions to "fill the earth" after the Flood. The Lord promised there would never be another flood to destroy the world, but these rebellious people built a tower reaching to the heavens in disbelief. The name Babel means "confusion" (v. 9) and refers to God's intervention by confusing the languages of the people.

The prophet Isaiah uses the king of Babylon as a symbol of Satan, who was once a covering cherub in heaven named Lucifer. In describing the downfall of Lucifer, he writes: "How you are fallen from heaven, O Lucifer, son of the morning! How you are cut down to the ground, you who weakened the nations!" (Isaiah 14:12). The book of Revelation most clearly uses the nation of Babylon as a symbol for Satan's reign.

The origins of Satan's kingdom began with his rebellion in heaven, which ended in a war when he was cast out. "War broke out in heaven: Michael and his angels fought with the dragon; and the dragon and his angels fought. ... So the great dragon was cast out, that serpent of old, called the Devil and Satan, who deceives the whole world; he was cast to the earth, and his angels were cast out with him" (Revelation 12:7, 9). This happened before the tower of Babel story.

Certainly the rebellious spirit of the people of Shinar and the same proud spirit in the king of Babylon capture the essence of Satan's kingdom. From the beginning of Satan's sin, he has sought to exalt himself above God. His reign has brought false worship, and his purpose has been to take captive the Lord's people. Every soul on Earth will finally line up on the side of either Jesus or Babylon. It is a matter of life and death!

THE NEW AGE

Will the New Age movement play a role in the
end-time conflict between good and evil?

"The serpent said to the woman, 'You will not surely die'"
(Genesis 3:4).

The New Age movement is really an old age movement that's been around since the devil first told Eve that she wouldn't die if she disobeyed God's command. The New Age movement has elements of older spiritual traditions that come from a wide range of "isms," including pantheism, polytheism, environmentalism, astrology, and many Eastern religions. It's really a hodgepodge of ideas that gained momentum in the 1960s and 70s when several "gurus" visited the United States.

There is a strong involvement in the New Age movement with the occult, psychic phenomena, and spiritism. Without a doubt, spiritism will be a major factor in the closing drama of Earth's history. Combined with the supernatural power of the counterfeit gift of tongues and allied with the end-time worldwide coalition of churches, spiritism will sweep the globe. The New Age belief in spirit communication and reincarnation is simply old-time paganism in new garb. Its belief in an immortal, undying soul that can communicate with the living is the same old falsehood Satan told Eve in Eden.

And books aren't the sole purveyors of this false religion. Television, film, and radio have been feeding society a steady diet of religious programming, most notably New Age spiritism. Shows like *Ghost Whisperer* and *Crossing Over* have a tremendous following, especially among young adults. Of course, the Harry Potter movies, aimed squarely at children, remain the standard for occult-oriented entertainment.

I know from personal experience that our only safety from being led astray is by personal Bible study. Without it, I might still be lost, perhaps steeped in the teachings of some New Age cult. It was the Bible that turned me into a Christian, which is kind of a miracle considering that I was a high school dropout from a Jewish family full of cynicism about Christianity. I'd been taught evolution and believed that the Bible was full of fiction and fantasy. Yet in a cave, all alone, I picked up the Bible and this dynamic, powerful book changed my life.

CAUGHT OFF GUARD

Is there really a danger that many Christians will be caught off guard when Jesus returns?

"Take heed to yourselves, lest your hearts be weighed down with carousing, drunkenness, and cares of this life, and that Day come on you unexpectedly" (Luke 21:34).

Jesus makes it very clear that several things can trap and destroy Christians. He even told a story to illustrate His warning: "It is like a man going to a far country, who left his house and gave authority to his servants, and to each his work, and commanded the doorkeeper to watch. Watch therefore, for you do not know when the master of the house is coming—in the evening, at midnight, at the crowing of the rooster, or in the morning—lest, coming suddenly, he find you sleeping" (Mark 13:34–36).

Let's consider the traps in Luke 21:34 along with Jesus' warning in Mark. The first item is "carousing." The original word comes from two Greek words, one for "head" and the other for "to sway or toss about." The idea is that we can become so busy in life, so intoxicated with our adrenaline-driven schedules, that we lose our ability to think clearly. This rat race of constant running keeps us from spending daily time with Jesus.

Drunkenness, of course, speaks of the result of drinking alcoholic beverages, but it can refer to any addiction. People who have numbed their minds through pornography, illicit sex, romance novels, gambling, alcohol, drugs, movies, food, or evil companions are clinging to dependencies that keep them from Bible study, prayer, and Christian fellowship. They live in an unreal world trying to fill a void in their life that only Jesus can truly fill. Even the everyday cares of this life can so consume us that we don't put first things first.

Finally, Mark 13 warns us that we can be spiritually asleep. It might be the biggest problem today. When a person is asleep, he doesn't really know he is asleep. Taking our relationship with Jesus for granted can make sleepwalkers of those who, unless miraculously wakened, will sleep past the moment of truth.

THE CHURCH

What does the word "church" mean?

"My sheep hear My voice, and I know them, and they follow Me" (John 10:27).

Have you ever been sitting in the bleachers, watching others play a game, and someone called out to you, "Hey, we're short one person—come join our side!" If you got up and joined their team, you became one of the "called out" persons. That's what the Greek word for church literally means. The word *ekklesia* comes from two words: "out" and "to call." Those who respond to Jesus' call become part of the church, which is also called "the body of Christ" (1 Corinthians 12:27).

In the secular Greek world, the word *ekklesia* described any group that gathered for a regular meeting, like a political rally. But in harmony with the Old Testament idea of a gathering or congregation, this word is especially applied to people who believed Jesus was the Messiah and chose to accept His teachings. They became part of a group and didn't just live in isolation. There was an emphasis on being part of the body (Romans 12:4, 5).

Unfortunately, the church became corrupt. Pagan teachings infiltrated the doctrines, and certain practices distorted the truth. The false church came to be called Babylon, and, in the last days, a call is made to "come out of her, my people, lest you share in her sins, and lest you receive of her plagues" (Revelation 18:4). This false church is also compared to an impure woman (v. 3), whereas God's true church and its followers are compared to a pure woman (Revelation 12:1).

How will you know if you are truly being "called out" to the right church? Study what the Bible says about God's true people. This group will share the everlasting gospel with the entire world (Revelation 14:6, 7). These people are called a "remnant" who remain loyal to God and keep all His commandments in the last days (Revelation 12:17). And these followers are filled with the faith of Jesus (Revelation 14:12).

Those who respond to God's call follow Peter's words to "repent and be baptized" (Acts 2:38). When people are baptized into the body of Christ, they become part of His church (1 Corinthians 12:13).

NEW DOCTRINES

Should we expect modern prophets to originate new doctrines?

"For I testify to everyone who hears the words of the prophecy of this book: If anyone adds to these things, God will add to him the plagues that are written in this book; and if anyone takes away from the words of the book of this prophecy, God shall take away his part from the Book of Life, from the holy city, and from the things which are written in this book" *(Revelation 22:18, 19).*

True end-time prophets will not originate new doctrine. The apostle John makes it clear that people who add or take away from the truth of Scripture are not being led by God. Any teaching that is not in harmony with the Word of God should be automatically dismissed. The Bible is the source of all doctrine, our sure foundation of truth. Isaiah warned, "To the law and to the testimony! If they do not speak according to this word, it is because there is no light in them" (Isaiah 8:20).

A true prophet is sort of like the moon, which reflects the sun. God's prophets do not lift themselves up, but point others to the Lord and encourage people to have a closer walk with Jesus. They do not direct attention to themselves but on the Bible. They are like smaller lights pointing people to the greater light of truth in the Word of God. Sometimes they reveal a deeper understanding of Bible doctrine that was clear during a certain time. "Surely the Lord GOD does nothing, unless He reveals His secret to His servants the prophets" (Amos 3:7).

God's prophets throughout time have helped protect His people from fanaticism, deception, and spiritual stupor. They have given direct messages to those who have turned from the Lord, rebuking, exhorting, and guiding them. Elijah confronted the prophets of Baal. Nathan challenged King David. Prophets helped to direct the early church.

John the Baptist prepared people for the first coming of Jesus. In the same way, God's last-day prophets will help people understand the end-time prophecies that indicate Christ is coming soon. Their messages are always in harmony with the Bible.

Sola Scriptura

If the Bible is the sole source of truth, shouldn't we reject all modern-day prophets?

"Do not despise prophecies. Test all things; hold fast what is good" (1 Thessalonians 5:20, 21).

I t is true that the source of all doctrine should be the Bible and the Bible only. But within the holy Scriptures, we are told that God gives the "gift of prophecy" to His church. The apostle Paul wrote, "He Himself gave some to be apostles, some prophets, some evangelists, and some pastors and teachers, for the equipping of the saints for the work of ministry, for the edifying of the body" (Ephesians 4:11, 12). Such gifts help to bring us all into "the measure of the stature of the fullness of Christ" (v. 13). If we say that we believe in the Bible and the Bible only, we must naturally accept what it teaches about the prophetic gift.

For instance, Jesus' end-time church will have the gift of prophecy (Revelation 12:17; 19:10; 22:9). Of course, we're told that we must test all prophets and, if they speak in harmony with the Bible, we should follow their counsel. Sometimes our pride is wounded when we are rebuked by a prophetic message. We turn away from the message and attack the messenger. We live in danger of ignoring truth we don't want to hear because we feel slighted.

Notice Jesus' words regarding the prophetic work of John the Baptist: " 'I say to you, among those born of women there is not a greater prophet than John the Baptist.' ... And when all the people heard Him, even the tax collectors justified God, having been baptized with the baptism of John. But the Pharisees and lawyers *rejected the will of God* for themselves, not having been baptized by him" (Luke 7:28–30, my emphasis).

Christians must follow the Bible's counsel regarding prophets. If I fail to listen to and test prophets, I am not basing my faith upon the Bible. Just remember that prophets who contradict God's Word are false and should be rejected.

MORE PROPHETS

Do you think more true prophets will appear between now and Jesus' second coming?

"It shall come to pass... that I will pour out My Spirit on all flesh; your sons and your daughters shall prophesy, your old men shall dream dreams, your young men shall see visions. And also on My menservants and on My maidservants I will pour out My Spirit in those days" (Joel 2:28, 29).

Based on Joel's prophecy, it certainly appears possible. Keep in mind that not all who call themselves prophets are true prophets. Jesus warns us there will also be false prophets. "Beware of false prophets, who come to you in sheep's clothing, but inwardly they are ravenous wolves" (Matthew 7:15). Genuine prophets focus on uplifting Jesus and the Bible. A false prophet is interested in consuming and gaining attention to themselves.

If someone in the last days claims to be a prophet, they should be tested by what the Bible says about true prophets. For instance, "Be diligent to present yourself approved to God, a worker who does not need to be ashamed, rightly dividing the word of truth" (2 Timothy 2:15). In addition to Christ's words about false prophets, He adds, "You will know them by their fruits. Do men gather grapes from thornbushes or figs from thistles?" (Matthew 7:16). When a person who freely breaks God's law claims to be a true prophet, we know they are deceived.

Many have distorted views of the work of God's prophets. They picture some type of carnival palm reader who makes predictions for money and to tickle the fancy of the curious. We are often drawn to the sensational. But when you compare that image with John the Baptist, it just doesn't match.

I believe God has already sent His remnant church a prophet in these last days to guide and direct His people in preparation for Jesus' soon return. Could the Lord send another prophet? Yes. I don't think we should box God in and make predictions that are not in harmony with Joel's vision. But if a person should be raised up, we should follow the advice of Paul, who wrote, "Do not despise prophecies. Test all things; hold fast what is good" (1 Thessalonians 5:20, 21).

STEWARDSHIP

What all is involved with proper Christian stewardship?

"God, who made the world and everything in it, since He is Lord of heaven and earth, does not dwell in temples made with hands. Nor is He worshiped with men's hands, as though He needed anything, since He gives to all life, breath, and all things" (Acts 17:24, 25).

Stewardship involves the proper handling of "all things" that we receive from God. The Lord gives us many types of blessings beyond money: "Every good gift and every perfect gift is from above, and comes down from the Father of lights, with whom there is no variation or shadow of turning" (James 1:17). Even our life, breath, and bodies are gifts we should care for. Stewardship simply means to carefully and responsibly manage something.

Our talents are given to us by God to use for building up the body of Christ. Spiritual gifts are distributed to all believers "from whom the whole body, joined and knit together by what every joint supplies, according to the effective working by which *every part does its share*, causes growth of the body for the edifying of itself in love" (Ephesians 4:16, my emphasis).

Time is a gift from God and should be used in doing the work the Lord has assigned each one of us. "It is like a man going to a far country, who left his house and gave authority to his servants, and to each his work, and commanded the doorkeeper to watch" (Mark 13:34). Are you using your time properly in witnessing for Christ (Acts 1:8)? In studying the Bible (2 Timothy 2:15)? In prayer (1 Thessalonians 5:17)? In helping those in need (Matthew 25:31–46)?

I like to think of stewardship as a partnership with God. Jesus has given me the assurance of salvation. He is my Savior and friend. As I walk with Him, I want to obey and follow Him as Lord of my life. That means submitting everything I have to be used for His glory. I hold nothing back from serving God. I acknowledge that He gave me my life, talents, time, family, money, and so much more to be used for His work.

HARD CHOICES

How do we handle those commands of God that seem unreasonable or too hard?

"Trust in the LORD with all your heart, and lean not on your own understanding; in all your ways acknowledge Him, and He shall direct your paths" (Proverbs 3:5, 6).

Children often feel that some of their parents' requirements are unreasonable. For example, "Don't play in the street" seems very restrictive to some kids. But in later years, the child will thank the parents for enforcing their rules.

We are "children" in dealing with God. He tells us, "For My thoughts are not your thoughts, nor are your ways My ways.... For as the heavens are higher than the earth, so are My ways higher than your ways, and My thoughts than your thoughts" (Isaiah 55:8, 9). Since He can see the end from the beginning, God very much knows the ultimate results of poor choices. He knows all the traps of temptation that could cause us harm. We need to trust our loving heavenly Father in the few areas we might not understand and stop "playing in the street" if that is what He asks of us.

God's rules are not arbitrary; they are for our benefit, to keep us from doing hurtful things. God wants only to bless us. The Bible says, "For the LORD God is a sun and shield.... no good thing will He withhold from those who walk uprightly" (Psalm 84:11). When we are truly in love with Jesus, we will give Him the benefit of the doubt and do His will even if we do not always understand why.

The new birth is the key. The Bible says that when I am truly born again, overcoming the world will not be a problem because a converted person will have the faith and trust to happily follow Jesus in everything. "For whatever is born of God overcomes the world. And this is the victory that has overcome the world—our faith" (1 John 5:4). Choosing to follow Him, even when we are not clear on His reasons, shows that our trust in our Savior is genuine.

MONEY AND PREACHERS

Are preachers today paid too much money
according to godly stewardship?

"The laborer is worthy of his wages" (Luke 10:7).

Yes, without doubt, many preachers are paid far more than they earn. Jesus said that "the laborer is worthy of his wages," but some preachers are receiving wages without being worthy. They have charisma but no character. You've probably noticed the seemingly arrogant flaunting of riches by some clergymen today; it's sad, but some seem to have put wealth above God.

This kind of attitude and behavior reduces the influence of all ministers. It brings reproach upon the name of Jesus. It causes hundreds of thousands to turn away in disgust from the church and its ministry. I fear such leaders will face an awful day of reckoning in the judgment. Preachers who are especially overpaid are likely to have widespread influence as well, and we all know there's truth to the adage, "Power corrupts."

What can Christians do to combat this problem? First of all, they can be very careful about who they support with their donations. Also, while avoiding judging others about their salvation, sometimes we need to speak out against a bad or corrupt situation.

Though the Christian church in general is not immune to overpaid preachers, I don't believe any minister in God's end-time remnant church is overpaid. All ministers receive virtually the same salary regardless of their job title or the size of their church. This eliminates a host of problems. In many cases, pastors' spouses work in the public marketplace to supplement these pastors' incomes.

Sadly, some people have pointed to overpaid preachers as an excuse to not return tithe. But we need to remember that the tithe is God's; regardless of who is on the receiving end, the person who returns their tithe will be blessed by the Lord. In Jesus' day, many of the priests were extremely corrupt, yet Jesus praised the woman who put two small coins into the temple treasury. Why? Because she gave her all in good faith; she was blessed for that.

LEGALISM

Is it legalistic to follow Christian rules of conduct?

"Beloved, do not imitate what is evil, but what is good. He who does good is of God, but he who does evil has not seen God" (3 John 1:11).

There is no legalism in doing what is right except when a person is doing it to curry favor for selfish reasons, instead of out of love for God. Of course, if they are trusting in their own deeds to save them, they are doomed to failure.

Salvation comes only as a miraculous, free gift from Jesus. The Bible says, "For by grace you have been saved through faith, and that not of yourselves; it is the gift of God" (Ephesians 2:8). We're saved by "grace," which means undeserved favor. None of us deserve the exquisite gift God has given us "while we were still sinners" (Romans 5:8). By putting our faith in Jesus, we are made right with God. He is the only one who can bridge the gap. Salvation by works (our conduct) is impossible.

But following Jesus' standards of conduct *because we have been saved and love Him* is never legalism. God asks us, 'Keep justice, and do righteousness, for My salvation is about to come, and My righteousness to be revealed" (Isaiah 56:1). We do what is right to honor the One who bought our salvation with His own blood. We do it because He said, "If you love Me, keep My commandments" (John 14:15). We obey out of love for our Savior.

Once we have been baptized into Christ, our lives should be very different. The apostle Paul puts it this way: "Our old man was crucified with Him, that the body of sin might be done away with, that we should no longer be slaves of sin. For he who has died has been freed from sin" (Romans 6:6, 7). The blood of Jesus breaks our chains and sets us free—not free to do whatever we please, but free from the slavery of doing what is wrong. He empowers us to do what is right.

CHRISTIAN PHARISEES

How can I adopt a Christian lifestyle without appearing judgmental or legalistic?

"These people draw near to Me with their mouth, and honor Me with their lips, but their heart is far from Me" (Matthew 15:8).

What makes a person pharisaical or legalistic is a lack of genuine love for God. Everything we do should be with one thought in mind: to express love and esteem for Jesus (1 John 3:22). When Christ is honored and reflected to others, they will be drawn to Him. Our question should always be, "Will this honor Jesus? Would I listen to this, sing this, do this, watch this, drink this, buy this, read this, say this, or go there if Jesus were here, in person, with me?"

Jesus *is* with us (Matthew 28:20), and His angels see everything we do. We must sense Jesus' presence in every facet and activity of life. When we consciously spend time with Him, we become like Him (2 Corinthians 3:18). Then when people are with us, they will respond as they did to the disciples of old: "They marveled. And they realized that they had been with Jesus" (Acts 4:13). Christians who live like that will never become pharisaical, judgmental, or legalistic.

In Old Testament days, God's people were in almost constant apostasy because they chose to live as their heathen neighbors rather than follow the distinctive lifestyle God outlined for them (Deuteronomy 31:16; Judges 2:17; 1 Chronicles 5:25). It is still true today. No one can serve two masters. Those who cling to the world's lifestyle will be slowly molded by Satan to adopt his feelings and desires and, thus, be programmed to be lost. Those who follow Jesus' principles will be changed into His image and will be prepared for heaven. There is no middle ground.

Jesus said, "He who does not take his cross and follow after Me is not worthy of Me" (Matthew 10:38). Following the Lord requires sacrifice, but what we sacrifice is microscopic compared to what we gain. The God of the universe wants to adopt us as His children and to love us forever. He wants to give us *everything!*

Fasting

Should Christians fast?

"When He had fasted forty days and forty nights, afterward He was hungry" (Matthew 4:2).

First, let's consider why Jesus fasted. Was it some form of self-abasement or torture? No. Jesus' fasting enabled Him to sharpen His focus on the things of God and His mission to save the world. While it temporarily weakened Him physically, it actually strengthened and braced Him spiritually. When the devil came with his temptations, Jesus was ready to overcome.

There are many other biblical precedents for fasting. Queen Esther, for example, fasted without food or water for three days when her people were threatened with extermination (Esther 4:16). Instead of feasting as a typical queen would, she put aside her own physical needs to fast, praying for the deliverance of her people. God heard her prayers and delivered them.

But should Christians tody fast? Jesus told His disciples that after He returned to heaven, there would be times when fasting would be appropriate. "The days will come when the bridegroom will be taken away from them; then they will fast in those days" (Luke 5:35). In addition, Jesus said there are some difficult challenges that can only be overcome when we pray and fast (Matthew 17:21).

While fasting is clearly taught in the New Testament, before doing so, you should carefully consider the state of your health. If you're in good health and are seeking guidance or a blessing, or have an urgent request for the Lord, fasting might be appropriate. There is no reason to believe that fasting for Christians is obsolete.

Remember also that fasting isn't always about abstaining from all food. It can mean abstinence from a variety of things. If for some reason you can't complete a food fast, you could consider a TV or media fast.

With the right attitude and humbleness of heart, fasting at proper times can be a form of worship and devotion to God, a way to seek His guidance and be drawn closer to Him.

Jesus' Atonement

How could one man's death pay the penalty for the sins of all mankind?

"For God so loved the world that He gave His only begotten Son, that whoever believes in Him should not perish but have everlasting life" (John 3:16).

A group of prisoners during World War II were put to work on an assignment under grueling conditions. The soldiers guarding them were brutal in their treatment; many of the captured were not even part of the enemy army.

One day the commander lined up the prisoners and stated that a shovel had been stolen and that the guilty party must step forward to be punished—which meant he would lose his life. After it was quiet for a moment, the commander shouted, "If someone doesn't step forward, I will kill all of you!"

At that moment a missionary quietly moved forward. The other prisoners gasped, because they knew this man had not stolen the shovel. They understood he was willing to give his life in order to save the rest of them. The missionary was indeed killed, and the men never forgot the sacrificial love of this innocent man.

In a small way, this story describes what happened when Christ stepped forward to give His life for a lost world. The pure, innocent Son of God willingly took the death sentence for all of us so that we, who rightfully deserve death, might be free. Romans 3:23 says, "All have sinned." Because "the wages of sin is death" (Romans 6:23) and all have sinned, something special was required for every person who has ever lived.

If Jesus was only a man, He could not have paid for the sins of the entire world; however, Jesus was all the fullness of God in a man's body (Colossians 2:9). Only one whose life is equal to all mankind could die for the sins of the human race. Because Jesus is the Creator and Author of all life, the life He laid down was more than equivalent to the lives of all people who would ever live. And since Christ rose from the dead, He is now able to administer the benefits of His gift of love to all who ask in faith.

GAMBLING

Does the Bible say it is wrong to gamble?

"A man with an evil eye hastens after riches, and does not consider that poverty will come upon him" (Proverbs 28:22).

In some ways, we take risks every day. Businessmen risk their livelihood on new products, for instance. But our subject today deals with something very different: the idea of placing a bet, or putting something of value at risk in order to win money or some other prize.

You won't find the word "gambling" in the Bible. So to answer this question, we need to look at biblical principles. In this regard, the Bible does make some strong statements indicating that "he who hastens to be rich will not go unpunished" (Proverbs 28:20). Most people who gamble to gain wealth end up with empty wallets. Take a look at these facts about gambling:

- Two-thirds of Americans have participated in some form of gambling.

- Compulsive gamblers are the lifeblood of casinos.

- About two-thirds of problem gamblers resort to crime to gain money for gambling or debts.

- People visiting Las Vegas double their risk of suicide.

California has almost a million problem gamblers, costing taxpayers about $1 billion annually due to the costs of criminal justice, unemployment, substance abuse, mental illness, and public assistance.

What about the lottery? This can be a temptation even for people who would never set foot in a casino. But, as with any form of gambling, the overwhelming majority loses money. The odds of making money through any form of gambling are very small. It's much better to save your money, wisely invest it, and to work. "He who has a slack hand becomes poor, but the hand of the diligent makes rich" (Proverbs 10:4).

Gambling is fueled by an overzealous desire for immediate wealth; people want to get rich quick. It's a natural desire, but that doesn't mean it's good. Greed is a trait that Christians should seek to eliminate from their lives; covetousness violates the tenth commandment. Remember, it was a love of silver that helped nail Jesus to the cross.

Finally, people who gamble are placing their faith in "remote chance"—a very unreliable companion. The only safe place to put your faith in is God. He will never let you down!

WILLPOWER AND GOD

How do I start doing what God wants me to do when I don't really want to do it?

"Therefore, to him who knows to do good and does not do it, to him it is sin" (James 4:17).

Once we know what God wants us to do, we need to take action and do it. Remember, though, that no one can make themselves "ready" to serve God. Only God can do that. Pray that He makes you willing to obey, to be filled with His love, and for His Spirit to work in your life. Then choose to obey Him right away!

Jesus said, "Not everyone who says to Me, 'Lord, Lord,' shall enter the kingdom of heaven, but he who does the will of My Father in heaven. Many will say to Me in that day, 'Lord, Lord, have we not prophesied in Your name, cast out demons in Your name, and done many wonders in Your name?' And then I will declare to them, 'I never knew you; depart from Me, you who practice lawlessness!'" (Matthew 7:21–23). Many feel they will be saved at Jesus' return, but they will, instead, be lost because they haven't obeyed God. They haven't known Jesus as their Friend or kept His commandments. They've only followed their feelings.

For the safety of our souls, we should never depend solely on feelings, because they are often deceiving. The devil can even influence our feelings. So if we depend on our feelings alone, he can more easily lead us to destruction. God would guide us through the unchanging words of Scripture. Our feelings, which can change on a whim, often lead us astray. Never listen to anything that contradicts the Holy Bible!

The Jewish leaders felt they should kill Jesus, but they were entirely wrong. They boasted about knowing the Scriptures, but they never took time to understand the only One who could save the human race. "Therefore whoever hears these sayings of Mine, and does them, I will liken him to a wise man who built his house on the rock" (Matthew 7:24). We need to build on that Rock!

BABIES IN HEAVEN

Will babies who die be saved in God's kingdom?

"Unless you are converted and become as little children, you will by no means enter the kingdom of heaven" (Matthew 18:3).

We don't have a specific answer to this question in the Bible, but some believe that infants will be saved based on a story that took place near the time of Christ's birth.

"Herod, when he saw that he was deceived by the wise men, was exceedingly angry; and he sent forth and put to death all the male children who were in Bethlehem and in all its districts, from two years old and under, according to the time which he had determined from the wise men. Then was fulfilled what was spoken by Jeremiah the prophet, saying: 'A voice was heard in Ramah, lamentation, weeping, and great mourning, Rachel weeping for her children, refusing to be comforted, because they are no more'" (Matthew 2:16–18).

It's a terribly sad story and shows the horrible lengths to which Satan went to destroy the Son of Man. Mothers who lost their babies sobbed because their children were "no more." But does this mean they will not see them in the resurrection?

The Old Testament foretold this tragic incident in Jeremiah 31:15. In speaking of the return of the exiles from Babylon, God spoke to mothers who lost children while being taken into captivity. The Israelite route passed through Ramah, and Matthew applies this reference to the mothers in Bethlehem who also cried for their children.

Notice what the next verse says: "Thus says the LORD: 'Refrain your voice from weeping and your eyes from tears; for your work shall be rewarded. ... and they shall come back from the land of the enemy. There is hope in your future, says the LORD, that your children shall come back to their own border'" (Jeremiah 31:16, 17). Could this be fulfilled in a greater sense, like many of the Old Testament prophecies, when Jesus returns?

I personally believe it is a reference to the future resurrection. When I consider the tender regard Jesus had for children, it is easy to picture angels carrying infants, raised back to life at the resurrection, and placed into their mothers' arms.

Sacrifices and Rewards

How can we know that the struggles and
sacrifices in this life are really worth it?

*"Blessed is the man who endures temptation; for when he has
been approved, he will receive the crown of life which the Lord
has promised to those who love Him" (James 1:12).*

The Bible is filled with encouraging words to help us persevere
and not lose heart. People in Bible times got discouraged and
needed a boost in their walk with God. The apostle Paul was
constantly challenged for his faith and could write to the church in
Rome: "And not only that, but we also glory in tribulations, knowing
that tribulation produces perseverance; and perseverance, character;
and character, hope" (Romans 5:3, 4).

The apostle Peter wrote to Christians who were suffering
persecution. He was not unaware of the problems his friends faced.
He later was martyred himself. But in the face of these trials, he stated,
"Be sober, be vigilant; because your adversary the devil walks about
like a roaring lion, seeking whom he may devour. Resist him, steadfast
in the faith, knowing that the same sufferings are experienced by your
brotherhood in the world. But may the God of all grace, who called us
to His eternal glory by Christ Jesus, after you have suffered a while,
perfect, establish, strengthen, and settle you" (1 Peter 5:8–10).

Paul cheered the church in Galatia to move forward through its
difficulties. He wrote: "Let us not grow weary while doing good, for in
due season we shall reap if we do not lose heart" (Galatians 6:9). Jesus
said, "Behold, I am coming quickly! Hold fast what you have, that no
one may take your crown" (Revelation 3:11).

One of Paul's strongest statements on whether the reward is
worth the sacrifice goes, "For I consider that the sufferings of this
present time are not worthy to be compared with the glory which
shall be revealed in us" (Romans 8:18). Just one glimpse of that eternal
kingdom will cause the worst trials and persecutions of Earth to pale
into insignificance, and the redeemed will cry out: "Hallelujah, heaven
is cheap enough!"

Heaven

Is heaven a misty place with souls who only play harps and float on clouds?

"Eye has not seen, nor ear heard, nor have entered into the heart of man the things which God has prepared for those who love Him" (1 Corinthians 2:9).

We cannot even begin to imagine the wonders and beauties of our future heavenly home. The apostle Paul could not find words to describe how special it will be. So where do distorted pictures of heaven come from?

This false teaching originated with the devil, the father of lies (John 8:44). He is anxious to twist God's loving plan and present heaven as an unreal, "spooky" place so people will lose interest or become skeptical of God's Word altogether. Satan knows that when people fully understand the Bible truth regarding the home of the saved, his power over them is broken, because they will begin making plans to enter that kingdom.

Will we be ghosts floating around in heaven? Not according to Jesus. After His resurrection, Christ proved to His disciples that He was flesh and bone by having them touch Him and by eating food. This very same Jesus ascended to His Father and will come again to Earth. The righteous will be given bodies just like the body of Christ and will be real people with flesh and bones throughout eternity. Our heavenly body will not be subject to death or decay.

The teaching that the saved in heaven will be ghosts who float on clouds and do nothing but play harps has no foundation in the Scriptures. Jesus did not die on the cross to provide any such trivial future. Most people have no interest in such an ethereal existence and, therefore, have little or no desire to enter God's heavenly kingdom—often preferring it only because they fear hell. If only all people everywhere could learn the truth about God's holy city and new earth, millions would begin to understand His love and would turn to Him with all their hearts. A person who misses out on God's kingdom has made the supreme blunder.

GREATEST DANGERS

What are the greatest dangers for Christians today?

"Do not be conformed to this world, but be transformed by the renewing of your mind, that you may prove what is that good and acceptable and perfect will of God" (Romans 12:2).

Obviously, there are many things in our world that threaten our relationship with God. Sometimes people fall rapidly from grace. At other times, moving away from truth happens in a subtle manner. One constant temptation for some—and among the greatest of dangers—is divided loyalties.

Many Christians have two loves that divide their hearts: love for Jesus, and love for the world and its sinful practices. Trying to satisfy both sides won't work. Jesus warned, "No one can serve two masters; for either he will hate the one and love the other, or else he will be loyal to the one and despise the other" (Matthew 6:24). We must choose one side.

God's Word says, "Do not love the world or the things in the world. If anyone loves the world, the love of the Father is not in him" (1 John 2:15). It is impossible to love the things that we know are wrong and still give our hearts to Jesus.

Still, too many people want to see how closely they can follow the world and still be considered Christians. They want the benefits of Christianity, but they also desire to conform to the world; they want to fit in and participate in its pleasures. People in this situation aren't being honest with themselves or with God. They are attempting to walk a narrow thread that doesn't exist.

In contrast, God tells us that we should "not be conformed to this world, but be transformed" (Romans 12:2). He wants us to be changed and conformed to the image of Christ, not the world. The Bible says, "For whom He foreknew, He also predestined to be conformed to the image of His Son, that He might be the firstborn among many brethren" (Romans 8:29). The Lord wants us to become like Jesus so we can be trusted in heaven.

FULLNESS OF ATONEMENT

Did Jesus make full atonement for all my sins—or must I do more?

"There is therefore now no condemnation to those who are in Christ Jesus" (Romans 8:1).

Christ did not make a partial payment for our sins when He died on the cross of Calvary. Jesus paid the full penalty for our transgressions. His gift was not just for a few good people, but for all. Those who accept Him in faith owe no works of penance for cleansing, but are already considered "washed" in the blood of the Lamb!

The teaching that we must perform penance implies there is a work we can do to help pay for our sins and thus earn our salvation. This belief is contrary to the Bible, which clearly states, "For by grace you have been saved through faith, and that not of yourselves; it is the gift of God, not of works, lest anyone should boast" (Ephesians 2:8, 9). A gift is not a gift if we make any payment for it.

I love how the prophet Isaiah describes this beautiful promise of forgiveness: "I, even I, am He who blots out your transgressions for My own sake; and I will not remember your sins" (Isaiah 43:25). This is more than a legal transaction. It's not just a matter of hitting the "delete" button on some heavenly computer! It's a promise of transforming power that will change our lives.

If we compare God to how most sinful people function, we might think the Lord would not forget our sins and that He would want to "make us pay" for breaking the law. But God is not like us. He is so much more. See how Micah describes the attitude of our Redeemer toward His people: "Who is a God like You, pardoning iniquity and passing over the transgression of the remnant of His heritage? He does not retain His anger forever, because He delights in mercy. He will again have compassion on us, and will subdue our iniquities. You will cast all our sins into the depths of the sea" (Micah 7:18, 19).

Divorce

Should we only support the innocent party
in a married couple getting a divorce?

"The LORD said to Samuel, 'Do not look at his appearance or at his physical stature, because I have refused him. For the LORD does not see as man sees; for man looks at the outward appearance, but the LORD looks at the heart'" (1 Samuel 16:7).

Too often when a couple has marital problems, others "take sides." It's easy to hear one side of a story but not know the other side. While it is true that there are cases in which one party has clearly broken a marital vow or has an out-of-control addiction that is destroying others, we should not overlook that a marriage is made up of two imperfect people.

I like to encourage concerned friends and families to focus less on "whose fault" caused the broken marriage and think more of how we can encourage healing and reconciliation. Instead of telling one party, "I'm praying for you," say, "I'm praying for you *both*." Humility should be the trademark of all Christians in how we deal with others, whether spouses, children, or fellow church members. The apostle Paul wrote, "Let nothing be done through selfish ambition or conceit, but in lowliness of mind let each esteem others better than himself" (Philippians 2:3).

The statistics are sobering about second marriages. Many "innocent" people in a divorce have not faced their own issues and turn around and marry another person who fits into their unhealthy way of functioning without even realizing it. When a person who suffers from divorce spends more time pointing a finger at the guilty party and does not realize they have issues in their own life, little progress will be made.

Sometimes the "innocent party," by lovelessness, inattentiveness, self-righteousness, unkindness, selfishness, nagging, and downright coldness, can encourage evil thoughts and actions in his or her spouse. Sometimes the "innocent party" might be equally as guilty before God as the "guilty" one. We are quick to make judgments about what seems "obvious" in others, but don't see the bigger picture. We can thank God that He looks more deeply at our motives and judges accordingly.

HELPING GOD

Is salvation really free?

"Everyone who thirsts, come to the waters; and you who have no money, come, buy and eat. Yes, come, buy wine and milk without money and without price" (Isaiah 55:1).

Imagine that it's your son's birthday. You've gone out and purchased him a gift, wrapped it up, and you hand it to him. He's excited as he rips off the wrapping paper and holds the present. He beams as he stares at it. Then he throws his arms around you and says, "Thanks! How much do I owe you?"

Of course, you say, "It's a gift. You don't owe me anything!"

Now picture yourself coming home from work and walking into the house. As you step into your bedroom to change, you notice an envelope on your dresser with your name on it. You tear it open and find money from your son's piggy bank with a little note that says, "Here's to pay for the present you gave me." You'd probably roll your eyes and think, *He doesn't get it. This is a gift. You're not supposed to pay anything for a gift!*

I know this story is a little far-fetched, but it illustrates Isaiah 55:1. The gifts of God are free. You receive them "without money and without price." There is nothing you can do to help God save you. Does salvation come with a price tag? Oh yes, but the amount is so large you could never purchase it. Only Jesus' life could pay for your sins and set you free. He gives you this gift as an act of grace that you may choose to receive by faith.

However, some people wrongly conclude that, because salvation is a free gift, they can ignore the law and abuse the privileges of grace. Not so. "Do we make void the law through faith? Certainly not! On the contrary, we establish the law" (Romans 3:31). When by faith we humbly repent of our sins and receive the gift of salvation, our response of love and obedience doesn't earn us eternal life, but demonstrates we have received the gift.

FAMILY CONFLICT

How do Christians deal with meddlesome parents and in-laws without dishonoring them?

"Aspire to lead a quiet life, to mind your own business, and to work with your own hands, as we commanded you" (1 Thessalonians 4:11).

As soon as a couple says, "I do," on their wedding day, they gain more than a new spouse. Their marriage increases their family to include in-laws. Having a new set of parents can be a wonderful experience, and many people develop close ties to their in-laws. Consider the close bond between Ruth and Naomi (Ruth 1:6). Yet it is also a transition that can be fraught with conflict and turmoil.

All parents feel some reluctance to let their children go. But if the apron strings are not cut, the new bond between spouses can be damaged. There is a sacred circle that should be around every home, and parents should not tamper with the union that exists exclusively between husband and wife. Parents should respect these boundaries and not tread where they are not invited.

Your goal as parents was to raise an adult, not keep your son or daughter in a state of being a dependent child. Here are a few suggestions: Pray for the spouses of your children, accept who they are, and only give advice when asked. Don't put your expectations on them, and allow them to make mistakes. Remember that you didn't raise a perfect child either.

But the married couple can also help in these situations by being patient. First, remember that your in-laws are not your parents, and don't put unrealistic expectations on them. Seek to understand their perspectives, and don't try to change them. Set healthy boundaries and have your spouse help out. The Bible says, "If it is possible, so far as it depends on you, live peaceably with all" (Romans 12:18).

There is a separation between parents and children that God ordained in the beginning. Jesus repeated this guide, as did the apostle Paul: "For this reason a man will leave his father and mother and be joined to his wife, and the two will become one flesh" (Ephesians 5:31). It would be well for parents and in-laws to respect God's counsel.

AGE FOR BAPTISM

How old should one be to qualify for baptism?

"He who believes and is baptized will be saved" (Mark 16:16).

Children should be old enough to understand the meaning of conversion and baptism. Of course, that age will vary from child to child. But let me emphasize that preparation for baptism is more than theoretically having knowledge of certain Bible teachings. People, whatever their age, should have a genuine conversion experience.

To those who heard the apostle Peter preach on the day of Pentecost and were "cut to the heart," he said, "Repent, and let every one of you be baptized in the name of Jesus Christ for the remission of sins; and you shall receive the gift of the Holy Spirit. For the promise is to you and to your *children*, and.... as many as the Lord our God will call'" (Acts 2:37–39, my emphasis). Children are capable of having a true religious experience with Jesus.

The Bible records instances in which entire families were baptized. I assume that includes some children who heard and responded to the gospel with their parents. Of the Philippian jailer, it says, "[Paul and Silas] spoke the word of the Lord to him and to all who were in his house. And he took them the same hour of the night and washed their stripes. And immediately he and all his family were baptized" (Acts 16:32, 33).

Children need to make an intelligent decision to surrender to Christ and follow Him. Many are ready for baptism at 10 or 11 years of age, some at 8 or 9. And some are not ready at 12 or 13. No age level is specified in the Bible, because children have different levels of experience and understanding. Some are ready earlier than others. It can be helpful to have young candidates write out a page or so on the topic, "Why I feel ready to be baptized."

You might wonder if a person should be old enough so that they will not slip and fall in their Christian experience. But adults slip and fall after baptism. A new Christian at whatever age is a "babe" in Christ. Everyone needs to be "born again"(John 3:3).

Biblical Reconciliation

Does God forbid reconciliation if one spouse ran off
with another person but later wants to return home?

*"Then the LORD said to me, 'Go again, love a woman who is
loved by a lover and is committing adultery, just like the love of
the LORD for the children of Israel, who look to other gods and
love the raisin cakes of the pagans'" (Hosea 3:1).*

One of the most amazing stories in all of Scripture is about a
prophet named Hosea who married a woman of ill repute.
She was unfaithful to her marriage vow many times, and God
asked Hosea to take her back. I'm not suggesting that God commands
every married person to take back a repentant spouse who has been
unfaithful. Jesus clearly taught us that divorce was permissible when
a partner has broken the marriage vow through adultery. Yet Hosea's
story does show us the incredible love and forgiveness that God
extends to us.

There is no hard rule in the Bible that states you should never take
back a repentant spouse who has been unfaithful. If such a spouse is
deeply repentant and exhibits a changed life over a period of time,
the other spouse, through much prayer and wise counsel, might
consider coming back together with their unfaithful partner. There
will be deep wounds to heal. Strong boundaries will need to be set in
place. The offending partner should be understanding of the pain and
distrust in their spouse.

A problem that can fester in the heart of any wounded person is
bitterness. Whether a spouse takes back their unfaithful partner or
not, God calls us to forgive others. Jesus said, "If you forgive men their
trespasses, your heavenly Father will also forgive you. But if you do
not forgive men their trespasses, neither will your Father forgive your
trespasses" (Matthew 6:14, 15). Forgiveness doesn't mean you forget
what happened or shove it under the carpet. But it does mean to let go
of the desire to pay the other person back.

I have personally seen the power of forgiveness bring healing to
marriages broken by unfaithfulness. It's not an easy road to walk, but
neither is a life of bitterness.

Salvation by the Law

Were people of the Old Testament saved by the law?

"[God] has saved us and called us with a holy calling, not according to our works, but according to His own purpose and grace which was given to us in Christ Jesus before time began" (2 Timothy 1:9).

No person has ever been saved by attempting to keep the law. In our own power, it is impossible and always has been from Adam all the way up to our time. All who have been saved in all ages have been saved by grace. As 2 Timothy 1:9 points out, this grace didn't begin at the cross but was established "before time began." The first gospel presentation was given after Adam and Eve sinned. The Lord said to the serpent, "I will put enmity between you and the woman, and between your seed and her Seed; He shall bruise your head, and you shall bruise His heel" (Genesis 3:15).

The law has many purposes. It is the basis of God's covenant (Exodus 20); it is our standard of judgment (Psalm 119:172); and it points out sin. The apostle James colorfully illustrates how the law is like a mirror that reveals sin in our lives (James 1:23–25). The law does not remove sin. Only Christ can save us from sin. The apostle Paul writes, "By deeds of the law *no flesh* will be justified in His sight, for by the law is the knowledge of sin" (Romans 3:20, my emphasis). This means every human being who has ever lived cannot be justified by trying to keep the law. Once you sin, it's just too late.

Some believe Jesus introduced grace on Earth. It is true that Christ provided the means of grace through His sacrifice, but such grace was extended to all mankind. Those before the cross looked forward to Jesus' atonement; those after the cross look back on it. Many in the Old Testament understood and received God's grace. Noah "found grace" (Genesis 6:8); Moses found grace (Exodus 33:17); the Israelites found grace (Jeremiah 31:2); and Abel, Enoch, Abraham, Isaac, Jacob, Joseph, and many other Old Testament characters were saved "by faith" according to Hebrews 11.

Domestic Violence

Does God expect me to live with a physically abusive spouse?

"Husbands ought to love their own wives as their own bodies; he who loves his wife loves himself. For no one ever hated his own flesh, but nourishes and cherishes it" (Ephesians 5:28, 29).

It is very sad that violence occurs in so many Christian homes. Statistically, it is almost always the husband abusing the wife, but it can happen the other way around as well. And there are many different ways family violence happens beyond physical abuse—psychological, emotional, sexual, and verbal. Physical abuse often happens in combination with other types of abuse. When we violate another person by hitting, kicking, slapping, punching, beating, or other forms of mistreatment, we devalue them as human beings created in God's image.

Sometimes Ephesians 5:22 is quoted to push wives to stay in an abusive relationship: "Wives, submit to your own husbands." The part that gets left off is "as to the Lord." So also this passage is looked over: "Husbands, love your wives, just as Christ also loved the church and gave Himself for her" (v. 25). It is in violation of Christian principles for a husband to demand his wife submit to his physical assaults to her or the children.

Unfortunately, there are times when a marriage deteriorates to a point where physical abuse calls for a separation. Physical harm can be life threatening and is a serious problem that demands immediate attention. The spouse and family members who have been physically abused must find a safe environment in which to live. Both husband and wife need to seek professional help through a qualified Christian marriage counselor. The goal is healing reconciliation, but that might not be reached in some of these cases.

It is in harmony with Christian principles for a spouse to seek a safe place and not live under physical abuse. Churches should be seen as havens of refuge and not be quick to question a person, typically a woman, who is struggling to be faithful in the marriage but is living under such cruelty. Some communities provide domestic violence shelters that give space and time for healing. Let us help those who are suffering from abuse and not ignore the problem.

HALLOWEEN

Should Christians be involved in Halloween?

"When they say to you, 'Seek those who are mediums and wizards, who whisper and mutter,' should not a people seek their God? Should they seek the dead on behalf of the living? To the law and to the testimony! If they do not speak according to this word, it is because there is no light in them" (Isaiah 8:19, 20).

It is believed that Halloween began as a pagan Celtic holiday. Many practices involved in this celebration were fed by superstition. The Celts believed the souls of the dead roamed the villages at night. Since not all the spirits were friendly, gifts and treats were left out to pacify the evil and to insure the next year's crop. They also dressed in costumes to confuse vengeful spirits. This practice eventually evolved into today's trick-or-treating.

Halloween is obviously not a holiday that Christians should celebrate. So what should Christians do at Halloween? Here are some guidelines:

Follow the Bible. Teach your children clearly that the Bible does not support worshiping the dead or trying to communicate with dead people. The Bible is clear that the dead are truly dead.

Share your faith. Instead of candy, share something appropriate to guide children toward Jesus and the Bible. "It is not the will of your Father who is in heaven that one of these little ones should perish" (Matthew 18:14).

Draw clear boundaries. Some activities at Halloween are obviously things a Christian will not participate in: watching horror movies, eating lots of junk food, playing pranks that hurt people, telling scary stories, or visiting so-called haunted attractions.

Refrain from a judgmental spirit. Perhaps your fellow Christians are not as clear or convicted as you are about how to deal with Halloween. Hurtful criticism will not help them. Instead of condemning parents, why not invite a few families into your home for a short Bible study, refreshments, and family-building games? Make it a time of worship and fellowship with the emphasis that, as Christians, the only thing we "hallow" is the name of our heavenly Father—to whom Jesus taught us when we pray to say, "Hallowed be Your name" (Matthew 6:9).

MODESTY

What does the Bible say about modesty?

"Abstain from every form of evil" (1 Thessalonians 5:22).

The problem of immodesty is always a two-way street. First, we live in an immoral society in which the prevalence of impurity, loose sexual conduct, and lack of boundaries is rampant. Insecure men often look for love in all the wrong places, and guys in bondage to pornography are led by their hormones to relate to women as objects to use, not as someone to respect and protect.

And it's not just guys who are being too aggressive. There seem to be fewer ladies who conduct themselves in modest and refined ways around young men. In the brokenness of our society, more and more children grow up with a giant hole in their heart. This hunger for love short-circuits their thinking, and they are led to grasp after feeling valued by others through destructive behaviors.

Let's consider the other side of the coin for a moment. Young women can carry themselves in such a way that can tempt young men to be too forward. A suggestive smile, revealing clothing, off-color comments or jokes, and even a "too relaxed" attitude can awaken temptation in a man. There is something about Christian reserve and dignity that helps remind a man to keep himself pure.

I encourage both young men and women to set healthy boundaries in their relationships with the opposite sex. Perhaps there are men you should never hang around. Learning to clearly say 'no' begins with a determination to follow the Bible's counsel to "make no provision for the flesh, to fulfill its lusts" (Romans 13:14). When you decide to go somewhere secluded with a person of the opposite sex telling yourself, "I'm not going to do anything wrong," you are only setting yourself up for failure.

Nurture purity in your conduct. Don't live in such a way that you feed the lust in your own heart or in the hearts of those around you. Carry yourself in a way that fulfills Jesus' counsel to "let your light so shine before men, that they may see your good works and glorify your Father in heaven" (Matthew 5:16). Is your life pointing others to Christ?

LAW OF LOVE

Does the New Testament replace the Ten Commandments with a new law of love?

"Love does no harm to a neighbor; therefore love is the fulfillment of the law" (Romans 13:10).

Some believe that God's Ten Commandments passed away at the cross. They quote Romans 13:10 to emphasize that He replaced the Decalogue with a new law—love. They say what God *really* wants from us is to love Him and others. But it's a redundant argument since the whole point of the Ten Commandments is to love God and love others.

Another text used to support this view is from a discussion Jesus had with a lawyer. The man asked which commandment was the greatest. Jesus said, " 'You shall love the LORD your God with all your heart, with all your soul, and with all your mind.' This is the first and great commandment. And the second is like it: 'You shall love your neighbor as yourself.' On these two commandments hang all the Law and the Prophets" (Matthew 22:37–40).

Christ did not replace the law by His statement, but revealed its deeper meaning. Just as your ten fingers are attached to your hands, God's commandments are all connected to the one great law of love. The essence of the first four commandments is to love God, and the spirit of the last six concerns how to love others.

Love fulfills the law by taking away the drudgery and making law-keeping a delight (Psalm 40:8). When we truly love a person, honoring his or her requests becomes a joy. Jesus said, "If you love Me, keep My commandments" (John 14:15). It is impossible to love the Lord and not keep His laws. The Bible says, "For this is the love of God, that we keep His commandments. And His commandments are not burdensome" (1 John 5:3).

To those who want to turn away from God's commandments, the Bible also says, "He who says, 'I know Him,' and does not keep His commandments, is a liar, and the truth is not in him" (1 John 2:4). Those are strong words for people who want to abolish God's eternal law.

DESTROY THE DEVIL

Why didn't God destroy the devil when he sinned and, thus, end the sin problem?

"The Lord passed before him and proclaimed, "The Lord, the Lord God, merciful and gracious, longsuffering, and abounding in goodness and truth, keeping mercy for thousands, forgiving iniquity and transgression and sin, by no means clearing the guilty" (Exodus 34:6, 7).

When sin first entered into the universe, it was something completely new, and it's likely the inhabitants did not fully understand it. Lucifer was a brilliant, highly respected angelic leader. His approach was one of great concern for heaven and the angels.

He probably said something like this: "Heaven is good, but it would be improved with more angel input. Too much unchallenged authority, as the Father and Son have, tends to blind leaders to real life. Angels should not be required to take orders. We should give the orders. God knows my suggestions are correct, and He is feeling threatened. Others will listen if we move in unison. We must not be weak; we must act."

Lucifer's arguments convinced many angels, and one-third joined him. If God had destroyed Lucifer immediately, some angelic beings who did not fully understand God's character might have begun to worship God through fear, saying, "Lucifer might have been correct. Be careful. If you differ with God, He might kill you." So nothing would have been settled. Instead, the problem would have been heightened.

The only service acceptable to God is voluntary service prompted by love. Obedience for any other reason is dangerous, futile, and doomed to fail. Satan claimed he had a better plan for the government of the universe. God gave him time to demonstrate its principles. The Lord will abolish sin only after every soul in the universe is fully convinced that Satan's government is unfair, hateful, ruthless, lying, and destructive.

KINGDOM COME

When will Christ set up His kingdom upon the earth?

"I saw a new heaven and a new earth, for the first heaven and the first earth had passed away. Also there was no more sea. Then I, John, saw the holy city, New Jerusalem, coming down out of heaven from God, prepared as a bride adorned for her husband" (Revelation 21:1, 2).

Jesus will set up His kingdom on Earth at the end of the 1,000-year period spoken of in Revelation 20. This chapter outlines events leading up to the establishment of His kingdom spoken of in the next chapter. After the second coming of Christ, Satan is bound to the earth for "a thousand years" (v. 2). During this time the righteous reign with Jesus in heaven for "a thousand years" (v. 4).

At the close of this 1,000 years "the holy city, new Jerusalem" (Revelation 21:2) comes down from heaven to the earth with all the saints (Zechariah 14:1, 4, 5) and the wicked dead of all ages are raised to life (Revelation 20:5). At this time, Satan will be released for "a little while" (v. 3) "to deceive the nations" (v. 8) and gather the wicked to make one last attack on "the camp of the saints" (v. 9). Of course, they will not succeed but be devoured by fire. But first there is a "great white throne" judgment, which is then followed by the final destruction of all sin and sinners in the lake of fire, which is "the second death" (v. 14).

When this fire comes down out of heaven and devours, it also purifies the earth and burns up all traces of sin and sinners (2 Peter 3:10), leaving only ashes (Malachi 4:3). Then God creates a new earth and gives it to the righteous. "God.... will dwell with them,.... and God Himself shall be with them, and be their God" (Revelation 21:3). Faultless, holy, happy beings, restored once again to the perfect image of God, will at last be at home in a sinless world as God originally planned. Only the most foolish person would choose to miss this!

QUIET PULPITS

Should we hear more teaching today about Christ's second coming?

"For the grace of God that brings salvation has appeared to all men, teaching us that, denying ungodliness and worldly lusts, we should live soberly, righteously, and godly in the present age, looking for the blessed hope and glorious appearing of our great God and Savior Jesus Christ" (Titus 2:11–13).

What is good news for some is bad news for others. When it comes to the second coming of Jesus, there is one for whom this spells disaster. The devil does not want people to know about, think about, or prepare for Christ's return. The "blessed hope and glorious appearing" of our Savior spells doom for this defeated enemy. His work to destroy God's people will end.

Until then, he continues to deceive and distract humans from this important Bible teaching by encouraging them to seek the traps of this world. Even many members of the church will not want to hear this special doctrine on Christ's coming. "For the time will come when they will not endure sound doctrine, but according to their own desires, because they have itching ears, they will heap up for themselves teachers" (2 Timothy 4:3).

Satan knows that the second coming is the "blessed hope" (Titus 2:13) of the Christian, and that once understood, it changes the lives of men and women and leads them to take a personal, diligent, and active part in spreading that good news to others so that Christ's coming may be hastened. This infuriates Satan, so he influences those who have "a form of godliness" (2 Timothy 3:5) but "denying its power," saying, "Where is the promise of His coming? For since the fathers fell asleep, all things continue as they were from the beginning of creation" (2 Peter 3:3, 4).

Those who deny, ignore, or make light of Christ's second advent (as a literal, soon-coming event) are specifically fulfilling Bible prophecy—and doing the devil a favor. But for the Christian, it is the grand climax of the gospel. Since we do not know the exact time of this event, we should be ready at all times.

HOLY SPIRIT

Did people have the Holy Spirit before the day of Pentecost?

"Jesus stood and cried out, saying, 'If anyone thirsts, let him come to Me and drink. He who believes in Me, as the Scripture has said, out of his heart will flow rivers of living water.' But this He spoke concerning the Spirit, whom those believing in Him would receive; for the Holy Spirit was not yet given, because Jesus was not yet glorified" (John 7:37–39).

There are many references in the Bible to the Holy Spirit working in the lives of people before the day of Pentecost. The Holy Spirit came upon Mary, the mother of Jesus (Matthew 1:18). John the Baptist was "filled with the Holy Spirit, even from his mother's womb" (Luke 1:15). David earnestly prayed, "Do not cast me away from Your presence, and do not take Your Holy Spirit from me" (Psalm 51:11). The Spirit worked in the days of Noah (Genesis 6:3) and on the heart of Joseph (Genesis 41:38).

The reference in the book of John speaks of a *special* outpouring of the Spirit promised on the day of Pentecost. After His resurrection, Jesus "commanded them not to depart from Jerusalem, but to wait for the Promise of the Father, 'which,' He said, 'you have heard from Me; for John truly baptized with water, but you shall be baptized with the Holy Spirit not many days from now'" (Acts 1:4, 5). The purpose of this special outpouring is explained: "But you shall receive power when the Holy Spirit has come upon you; and you shall be witnesses to Me in Jerusalem, and in all Judea and Samaria, and to the end of the earth" (v. 8).

The fact that a special gift of the Spirit was promised by Christ to the disciples at the launching of the church does not mean the Holy Spirit did not work previous to this time. It simply points to an extra measure to help start the work of evangelizing the whole world. Before Christ comes, a similar but greater outpouring of the Spirit, called the "latter rain," will be given to help complete the gospel work (see Joel 2:23 and James 5:7).

Honoring Unconverted Parents

Should we still honor our parents if they are abusive?

"Honor your father and your mother, that your days may be long upon the land which the LORD your God is giving you" *(Exodus 20:12).*

All of the commandments are a reflection of God's loving character, so I don't believe we can safely ignore any of them, regardless of the circumstances.

However, we need to understand what honoring our parents really means. It doesn't necessarily mean condoning all their actions. Abuse in any form is wrong, evil, and against the principles of Scripture. That said, there is a certain inherent respect that should always be shown to a parent. Even when we disagree with them, we can do it respectfully.

I do believe that where abuse is involved, a person can respect a parent and still take action against that parent, such as the time King Asa removed his mother from power because she had set up an idol (2 Chronicles 15:16).

Obviously, if a parent asks you to break one of God's commandments, you should decline. God must be honored above a parent.

Sometimes it might be necessary for adult children to keep a distance for a time, especially if the parent continues the abusive behavior or if you're clashing continuously. Separation is also appropriate when parents are meddling, perhaps trying to interfere in the raising of a grandchild or in the marriage (see Genesis 2:24).

However, we should avoid cutting off all ties with our parents if it's possible to retain some type of cordial relationship. "I never want to see you again," is pretty harsh and usually unnecessary. People change—they change and we change. As a Christian, you want to have a redemptive relationship and learn how to resolve conflict.

Being a Christian means sometimes you have to be kind and loving to people who aren't lovable. Jesus said, "Love your enemies, bless those who curse you, do good to those who hate you, and pray for those who spitefully use you" (Matthew 5:44). Through the grace and power of Christ, the Christian can show mercy even to those who "spitefully use" them.

BECOMING ANGELS

Do people become angels when they die?

"As Peter knocked at the door of the gate, a girl named Rhoda came to answer. When she recognized Peter's voice, because of her gladness she did not open the gate, but ran in and announced that Peter stood before the gate. But they said to her, 'You are beside yourself!' Yet she kept insisting that it was so. So they said, 'It is his angel'" (Acts 12:13–15).

When the apostle Peter was miraculously delivered from prison, the young lady, Rhoda, who answered the door could hardly believe it was him. In her excitement, she left Peter locked outside and rushed to tell the others. Since he had been previously delivered by an angel, the other believers in the house praying for Peter's release apparently thought this might be his angel.

It is not strange that these followers of Jesus believed Rhoda saw a spiritual being. Even Christ's disciples had moments when they thought they were seeing some type of spirit. When Jesus came to them on the water during a storm, it says, "When they saw Him walking on the sea, they supposed it was a ghost, and cried out" (Mark 6:49). After the resurrection, Jesus' appearance alarmed some. "As they said these things, Jesus Himself stood in the midst of them, and said to them, 'Peace to you.' But they were terrified and frightened, and supposed they had seen a spirit" (Luke 24:37).

Some people believe Acts 12:15 indicates that when people die they immediately become angels. During the time between the Old and New Testaments, many interesting theories about angels were formulated by Jewish teachers.

But the Bible teaches that angels are not of the same order as human beings (Psalm 8:5) and existed before people were even created (Job 38:4–7). Before any person ever died angels existed in the garden of Eden (Genesis 3:24). God has provided each of His children a guardian angel (Matthew 18:10; Psalm 34:7). Someday God's angels will come and gather the Lord's people at the second coming of Jesus (Mark 13:27).

EFFECTIVE PRAYER

What can I do or say so that my prayers are actually answered?

"If you then, being evil, know how to give good gifts to your children, how much more will your heavenly Father give the Holy Spirit to those who ask Him!" (Luke 11:13).

One of the first things I remind people who ask me this question is that we have a loving Father who wants to answer our prayers and give us good things. Sometimes people have the idea that God is reluctant or irritated when we come seeking answers or help. But this just isn't true. The Lord deeply cares about us and is delighted when we pray to Him. We can also have confidence that God hears us (1 John 5:14, 15).

Can we do things that increase the likelihood of God answering our prayers? The Bible addresses this across many verses. First of all, when we approach the Lord in prayer, we should be like Jesus, who said, "O My Father, if it is possible, let this cup pass from Me; nevertheless, not as I will, but as You will" (Matthew 26:39). We must be willing to give up our ideas about answered prayer and put all things into God's hands.

Don't hesitate to bring anything that troubles you to the Lord. "Casting all your care upon Him, for He cares for you" (1 Peter 5:7). Prayer is a time in which we can roll our burdens into the hands of a loving God. Mix praise and thanksgiving into your prayers. "In everything give thanks; for this is the will of God in Christ Jesus for you" (1 Thessalonians 5:18).

Something I've found helpful is to find a quiet place where I am not interrupted by the busy things that often press on me. Jesus did this: "Now in the morning, having risen a long while before daylight, He went out and departed to a solitary place; and there He prayed" (Mark 1:35). I think it also helps to have times when you pray aloud. The disciples often heard Christ pray (Luke 11:1). As we pray in faith, even if the answer is no, we can know that God hears us and cares.

CAIN'S WIFE

Where did Cain find a wife?

"Cain knew his wife, and she conceived and bore Enoch. And he built a city, and called the name of the city after the name of his son—Enoch" (Genesis 4:17).

As we read the story of Cain's fall in Genesis 4, it seems as if the time frame between verse 16 and 17 is only a couple of days. Though the story doesn't indicate this, some have wondered if Cain somehow found a wife who came from people other than Adam and Eve. They conjecture that perhaps somewhere else on Earth God also created Alfred and Elaine. But there is no Scripture passage to support this notion.

As Adam and Eve followed God's command to "be fruitful and multiply" (Genesis 1:28), they had many children. They were not encumbered with the degeneration brought about by sin that we see today. Not only did they live much longer lives, but also the genetic deficiencies seen today when close relatives marry and bear children did not exist. So Cain's wife would obviously be from the offspring of Adam and Eve. Brothers and sisters must have married.

The same question is raised regarding the children of Noah who survived the worldwide flood. Cousins must have married since there were no other people on the earth. Even up to the time of Abraham, we find close relatives marrying; Sarah was his half-sister. But as the effects of sin have multiplied, there is a greater risk of couples sharing recessive gene traits that can lead to an increase in birth defects. Eventually, God banned the practice.

There are a variety of laws concerning marrying first or second cousins across our planet. In some places it is encouraged, while in others it is illegal. Interestingly, the Bible speaks to this issue. "None of you shall approach anyone who is near of kin to him, to uncover his nakedness: I am the LORD" (Leviticus 18:6). The list of examples given in the text apparently does not include cousins. Examples of first cousins getting married can be found in Scripture, such as the marriage of Isaac and Rebekah (Genesis 24:12–15).

NATURAL DISASTERS

Does God cause natural disasters?

"It is not the will of your Father. ... in heaven that one of these little ones should perish" (Matthew 18:14).

It seems logical that if God is all powerful, He must be responsible for everything that happens on our planet. But there is a missing piece we must not overlook: Both good and evil exist in our world. There are flowers and thorns, fresh air and pollution, love and hatred.

Why? The devil was once Lucifer, a being who stood by the throne of God. He became jealous and began to spread rumors that God was selfish, controlling, and unjust. The accusations grew until Satan and a third of the angels were cast out of heaven to the earth (Revelation 12:7–9). Instead of immediately destroying the devil and creating confusion and fear in the hearts of all the other beings, the Lord allowed Satan to play out his ideas before the watching universe.

After Adam and Eve sinned, the world began to change (Genesis 3:17). The enemy was permitted to touch our planet and bring destruction through earthquakes, tornados, fires, and floods. As we come closer to the end of time, Jesus predicted these types of events will increase (Matthew 24:8). But God has not abandoned His people.

When Jesus came, He brought healing and hope. "The Son of Man did not come to destroy men's lives but to save them" (Luke 9:56). To questioning and blaming people, He once said, "Many good works I have shown you from My Father. For which of those works do you stone me?" (John 10:32). Evil does not come because God is unfair. It often comes because God is pushed away. "And many evils and troubles shall befall them, so that they will say in that day, 'Have not these evils come upon us because our God is not among us?'" (Deuteronomy 31:17).

Yet sometimes innocent people suffer in this world of sin. Calamity does not always come to sinful people. Jesus more than once corrected that false teaching (see Luke 13:1–5). Catastrophes will not last forever. Christ promised to come and put an end to all calamities.

Biblical Wisdom

How can I become wise like Solomon?

"If any of you lacks wisdom, let him ask of God, who gives to all liberally and without reproach, and it will be given to him" (James 1:5).

One of the most encouraging verses in the Bible on finding help is found in James 1:5. The apostle James doesn't limit this promise to a certain group, but says, "If *any* of you lacks wisdom ..." Furthermore, when we ask God for help, he writes that the Lord gives *liberally and without reproach*. God is not only generous in helping us, but He does not express disappointment with such requests. The Lord is delighted when we come seeking His guidance.

It's also worth taking note that James says, "If any of you lacks *wisdom* ..." The Greek word for wisdom is *sophia,* which is more than intellectual knowledge. Sometimes when looking for help in our lives, we seek for ideas that might only touch the surface of a problem. Wisdom goes deep and provides insight into overlooked factors, such as our motives.

One of my favorite ways to approach Bible study is to discover Christ in all the Bible. An interesting way Jesus is presented in Scripture is through a connection with wisdom. Christ embodies wisdom. The apostle Paul describes Jesus as "the power of God and the wisdom of God" (1 Corinthians 1:24). The book of Proverbs regularly speaks of wisdom as a person (Proverbs 1:20; 8:1; 9:1–5). And so Christ is the source of all wisdom.

When seeking God's guidance, take time to search your heart and confess any known sin that might prevent God's blessing (Psalm 66:18). Think of your motives (James 4:3), have faith that the Lord can lead you (Psalm 32:8), and seek counsel from godly people (Proverbs 11:14).

Finally, be open to different ways God might be directing you. We call these "providences." These are signs or indications of how the Lord could be opening or closing doors. It might be a special Bible verse, a comment from a Christian friend, or an opening pathway.

Pride and Self-Esteem

What does the Bible say about low self-esteem?

"But as many as received Him, to them He gave the right to become children of God, to those who believe in His name" (John 1:12).

While the Bible warns us to not think of ourselves more highly than we ought, there are some who deny the value God places on each of us as His children. People who struggle to have a healthy perspective about themselves often have experienced serious pain from rejection in their lives. The Bible reminds us, "You are a chosen generation, a royal priesthood, a holy nation, His own special people, that you may proclaim the praises of Him who called you out of darkness into His marvelous light" (1 Peter 2:9).

We need to remember that a loving heavenly Father brought us life. When we give our lives to Him, we are adopted into His family. John 1:12 tells us that when we receive Christ, we are given the "right" to become God's children. What a high privilege!

There is no one else in all the universe just like you. He saw you before you were born. "For You formed my inward parts; you covered me in my mother's womb. I will praise You, for I am fearfully and wonderfully made" (Psalm 139:13, 14). The Lord personally knows you. "Fear not, for I have redeemed you; I have called you by your name; You are mine" (Isaiah 43:1).

"But," you say, "you don't understand. God cannot love me. You don't know what I've done, where I've been, and what I am really like deep down inside. My background is so broken, my body is deformed, and my personality is simply obnoxious. God loves nice people, but He couldn't love me." To such people I would say, "Not according to the Bible."

Notice the word of the apostle Paul: "For I am persuaded that neither death nor life, nor angels nor principalities nor powers, nor things present nor things to come, nor height nor depth, nor any other created thing, shall be able to separate us from the love of God which is in Christ Jesus our Lord" (Romans 8:38, 39). Yes, God really does love you!

Living in Fear

How can I live with more confidence?

"There is no fear in love; but perfect love casts out fear, because fear involves torment. But he who fears has not been made perfect in love. We love Him because He first loved us" (1 John 4:18, 19).

It is not God's plan for you to live in constant fear. It can paralyze you from making good choices or facing difficult circumstances. You are not alone when it comes to feeling fear, anxiety, or worry. And not all fear is bad. It can keep us on alert for possible dangers around us. The Lord created us with a "fight or flight" response to help keep us safe. The problem with fear is when it becomes unmanageable or unreasonable.

One of God's most courageous men in the Bible was afraid. King David faced many giants in his life. Goliath and King Saul wanted to take his life. He once wrote, "Whenever I am afraid, I will trust in You. In God...I have put my trust; I will not fear. What can flesh do to me?" (Psalm 56:3, 4). The key to coping with fear for David was trust. He put his fears in perspective by remembering the power of God to protect him.

Nothing can melt our fears like keeping God's love in our minds and hearts. The Bible teaches us that when love abides in the heart, fear is cast out. Solomon also reminds us, "When you lie down, you will not be afraid; yes, you will lie down and your sleep will be sweet. Do not be afraid of sudden terror, nor of trouble from the wicked when it comes; for the LORD will be your confidence and will keep your foot from being caught" (Proverbs 3:24–26).

When your fears seem overwhelming, stop and pray. Breathe deeply and slowly, asking God to surround you with His love. Write down and memorize key Bible verses about fear. "Yea, though I walk through the valley of the shadow of death I will fear no evil; for You are with me; Your rod and Your staff, they comfort me" (Psalm 23:4).

SABBATH VS. CAREER

How do I keep the Sabbath when
I have a work conflict?

"Seek first the kingdom of God and His righteousness, and all these things shall be added to you" (Matthew 6:33).

Members of Sabbath-keeping churches observe the seventh day as God's holy rest day, from sundown on Friday evening until sundown on Saturday evening. During this time, according to the commandment, they put away all unnecessary work in order to worship and keep the Sabbath holy. It is not a day to catch up at home on odd jobs or engage in secular amusements, but it is sacred and devoted to God.

One of the best ways to deal with Sabbath work issues is to write a letter to your employer explaining your decision to become a Sabbath-keeper. Share that it is your religious conviction to observe God's Sabbath and that it would be a violation of your beliefs to work during those hours. According to Title VII of the Civil Rights Act and the guidelines of the Equal Employment Opportunity Commission in the United States, accommodation should be made for you.

Show a willingness to work with your employer on a solution that works for both of you. For instance, you can offer to work on Sundays, holidays, or evenings to cover these hours. Seek to cooperate and show that you have an interest in the company and appreciate working for them. Offer to come in and talk further with them if that would help.

Most pastors will assist you in giving counsel and writing such a letter. Many Sabbath-keeping churches also have a religious liberty director who is dedicated to supporting a person in your circumstances, as well as those being asked to take exams on Sabbath or if a person has a new employee who creates challenges.

Laws vary in different countries and existing laws in your country can change. There will come a time when governments and religious organizations will take away freedom and seek to coerce people to worship against their convictions. True Christians will stand for their faith and on the Word of God, no matter the consequences. The Lord promises to watch over us in these trying times.

Jewish Dietary Laws

Aren't health laws in the Old Testament only intended for the Jews?

"Whether you eat or drink, or whatever you do, do all to the glory of God" (1 Corinthians 10:31).

God's health laws are actually found all over the Bible. In the New Testament, we read, "Beloved, I pray that you may prosper in all things and be in health, just as your soul prospers" (3 John 2). The Scriptures show a high priority in caring for our health. God gave us these guidelines because He knows what is best for the human body. "The LORD commanded us to observe all these statutes, to fear the LORD our God, for our good always, that He might preserve us alive" (Deuteronomy 6:24).

Jesus' death on the cross redeems us from sin, but it did not change what is deemed healthy or un- healthy. If pork is listed as something unhealthy before Christ died, it doesn't really make sense that Calvary suddenly makes eating swine's flesh healthy. Actually, the notion of "clean" and "unclean" animals goes all the way back to Genesis, long before there were any Jews. Noah was given instructions about clean and unclean animals (see Genesis 7:2); he wasn't a Jew.

We wrongly assume that our walk with God is somehow a spiritual-only exercise that has nothing to do with our lifestyle. But as our text points out, the Lord is interested even in what we eat and drink. God doesn't create meaningless rules to make our lives miserable. He loves us. "No good thing will He withhold from those who walk uprightly" (Psalm 84:11).

Modern science confirms that the guidelines in Leviticus 11 and Deuteronomy 14 provide a diet that lowers the chance of disease. If we eat meat, we are taught to eat only those animals that have a split hoof and chew the cud, and fish that have both fins and scales, and to avoid birds of prey. A Christian will guard his appetite and not consume things like hogs, squirrels, rabbits, catfish, eels, lobsters, clams, crabs, shrimp, oysters, and frogs.

The apostle Paul reminds Christians: "Do you not know that you are the temple of God and that the Spirit of God dwells in you?" (1 Corinthians 3:16). It's still good advice.

FAITH AND LONELINESS

What can a Christian do when feeling deep loneliness?

"Behold, I am with you and will keep you wherever you go, and will bring you back to this land; for I will not leave you until I have done what I have spoken to you" (Genesis 28:15).

One day, Jacob deceived his father in order to receive the birthright from his older brother. Now his life was in danger, so his mother sent him away. As he laid down that first night on the ground, using a stone for a pillow, he felt very alone. Then God spoke to him the words in Genesis 28. The warmth of the Lord's promise assured Jacob that he wasn't really alone. God came close.

Elijah was afraid of a wicked queen who threatened to kill him. He ran into the wilderness and wished he would die. Finally, while Elijah hid in a lonely cave, God came close and spoke words of comfort to a man who *thought* he was alone. In a still small voice, the Lord assured lonely Elijah that he was not forsaken (see 1 Kings 19).

Jesus understands your feelings of loneliness. "He is despised and rejected by men, a Man of sorrows and acquainted with grief. And we hid, as it were, our faces from Him; He was despised, and we did not esteem Him" (Isaiah 53:3). We can be assured that the Lord will not abandon us. "For He Himself has said, 'I will never leave you nor forsake you'" (Hebrews 13:5).

Some people feel alone when they go through a divorce, their spouse dies, or they break up with someone special. But God makes this promise: "Do not fear, for you will not be ashamed; neither be disgraced, for you will not be put to shame; for you will forget the shame of your youth, and will not remember the reproach of your widowhood anymore. For your Maker is your husband, the LORD of hosts is His name" (Isaiah 54:4, 5).

Out of the fullness of God's love being poured into your heart, do not withdraw. Reach out to others. Invest your life in bringing happiness to those around you. Seek to make friends and cultivate healthy social connections.

INTERCESSION

Does it really make a difference to pray on behalf of other people?

"Pray for one another, that you may be healed. The effective, fervent prayer of a righteous man avails much" (James 5:16).

I believe in the power of intercessory prayer, not only because I have seen God work in powerful ways to change lives, but also because the Bible repeatedly gives us instruction on how we should pray for others.

Many Bible heroes were intercessors. Abraham interceded for Sodom (Genesis 18), Moses cried out for Israel (Exodus 32), as did David, Samuel, Hezekiah, and others. Jesus is our great Intercessor, and all of our prayers go through Him. "There is one God and one Mediator between God and men, the Man Christ Jesus" (1 Timothy 2:5).

One of the clearest models of intercessory prayer is found in Daniel 9. Here we read how this Old Testament prophet poured out his heart on behalf of his people. Like a type of Christ, Daniel identifies with the sins of the people, using the word "we" repeatedly in this prayer. He takes this time of intercession seriously by fasting and taking off his government work robes.

The Bible tells us the different types people for whom we should intercede, such as those in authority (1 Timothy 2:2), the church (Psalm 11:6), friends (Job 42:8), the sick (James 5:14), and even those who persecute us (Matthew 5:44). It doesn't take a special calling to intercede for others. All Christians should pray for their family and friends and those in need.

My favorite story that demonstrates the power of intercessory prayer is the apostle Peter's release from prison by an angel. Notice how Luke introduces this incident: "Peter was therefore kept in prison, but constant prayer was offered to God for him by the church" (Acts 12:5). In this case, the answer to the prayers of the church for Peter's release was a resounding 'yes.'

We might be tempted to think that intercessory prayer is a waste of time because we don't always "get" what we have prayed for. But we should remember to ask for God's will to be done. Sometimes that means 'no' and sometimes it means "wait."

HAUNTED BY THE PAST

What does the Bible say about old wounds and bad experiences from my past?

"When I was a child, I spoke as a child, I understood as a child, I thought as a child; but when I became a man, I put away childish things" (1 Corinthians 13:11).

Many adults struggle with pain and scars from their childhood. The abuse some people experienced growing up in a home filled with violence, abuse, neglect, or parents who had addictions is not a simple matter to "put away." Some of these hurts go very deep, and the natural response is to cover them with unhealthy substances like drugs and alcohol or unhealthy behaviors. The problem is that you don't just flip a switch and forget about such things. It's like taking your garbage and sticking it in a closet in your house. Pretty soon your whole house stinks.

God's plan is to bring healing to your wounded heart. We all want to forget about these things. But how do you "put away childish things"? We need to be honest about our past. We can't fool ourselves or say nothing ever happened. That's not being truthful. Paul counsels, "Therefore, putting away lying, 'Let each one of you speak truth with his neighbor,' for we are members of one another" (Ephesians 4:25). There are many steps that can help you with this process. Sometimes a Christian friend or counselor can walk you through letting go.

Sometimes people overlook the role of forgiveness in facing their past. They stew in continued anger toward parents or others who hurt them. They feel justified in being angry, but it only traps them more deeply in bitterness and spoils their life. We will be free when we forgive "one another, even as God in Christ forgave you" (Ephesians 4:32). This doesn't mean we completely forget what happened, but it no longer becomes a central focus in our minds.

God has a purpose for our lives and can take all things, even the pain from our past, and make it into something beautiful in His time (Ecclesiastes 3:1, 11). He promises to heal our broken hearts and give us "beauty for ashes" (Isaiah 61:3).

WANDERING CHRISTIANS

How can I help a friend who has quit attending church?

"As we have opportunity, let us do good to all, especially to those who are of the household of faith" (Galatians 6:10).

Most people who quit church do so because of a relational issue within the congregation or they are trying to cope with a challenging situation. Some do leave because of doctrine, but the majority have had a conflict with someone in the church or something happened in their life that is leaving them discouraged. It might be that they lost their job, are going through a divorce, had a car accident, or are taking care of an ill relative.

When people stop attending church, many of them are wondering if the church really cares about them. They might be discouraged with their own failures, but they might also focus on the lack of genuine love coming from others. Of course, this all begins to take a toll on their spiritual life. Bible study and prayer time can start to slip. They begin to question whether church is even relevant to their lives anymore.

That's why it's important for members to take initiative and reach out to missing members. Like the parable of the lost sheep in Luke 15, Jesus pursues those who wander away.

When making contact with someone who has stopped coming to church, put away any critical or condemning attitudes you might have and focus on being kind and understanding. If they are going through a difficulty, try listening without being judgmental. It might be tempting to start lecturing them on their lifestyle, but it would be better to demonstrate love and acceptance at this starting point.

You might eventually ask a couple of open-ended questions. "Tell me about growing up in the church. What was it like for you?" Another question is, "I understand you used to attend church. I'm interested in what led to you stopping."

Eventually you can share your own story of coming to know Jesus and what the church means to you. You can share appropriate literature with them or even get together with them outside of church. At some point, as the Holy Spirit leads you, you can invite them to come back.

Fractured Church

Why are there so many denominations if they all claim to follow Jesus?

"In that day seven women shall take hold of one man, saying, 'We will eat our own food and wear our own apparel; only let us be called by your name, to take away our reproach'" *(Isaiah 4:1).*

The fact that you call an orange an apple doesn't make the orange an apple. In Isaiah 4:1, the seven women say they will eat their own food and wear their own apparel, yet they want to take a man's name. It reminds me of how truth has been compared to food—or bread—in John 6:35 and apparel is a symbol of righteousness in Revelation 19:8. How many churches call themselves by the name Christian but don't uphold the bread of truth and teach us to wear Christ's robe of righteousness?

God's church is defined by the apostle Paul as the pillar of truth. He wrote Timothy on how people "ought to conduct" themselves "in the house of God, which is the church of the living God, the pillar and ground of the truth" (1 Timothy 3:15). If a denomination is not teaching truth, it is not truly God's church.

Daniel predicted that a time would come when a religious power would "cast truth down to the ground" (Daniel 8:12). Paul warns, "Let no one deceive you by any means; for that Day will not come unless the falling away comes first, and the man of sin is revealed" (2 Thessalonians 2:3).

We should expect there to be false churches that do not teach truth from Scripture but teach "as doctrines the commandments of men" (Matthew 15:9). Otherwise, why would Paul encourage us to "test all things; hold fast what is good"? (1 Thessalonians 5:21).

The book of Revelation speaks of God's end-time church and gives us indicators for knowing if a denomination is truly following the Lord. Of this remnant people, the apostle John writes, "The dragon was enraged with the woman, and he went to make war with the rest of her offspring, who keep the commandments of God and have the testimony of Jesus" (Revelation 12:17). God's true church stands on biblical truth.

MARY, MOTHER OF JESUS

Does the Bible teach us to pray to
Mary, the mother of Jesus?

"His mother [Mary] said to the servants, 'Whatever He says to you, do it'" (John 2:5).

There are many religions in the world in which people pray to idols or pagan gods and claim their prayers are answered. I do not believe that is proof enough or is sufficient criteria to determine whether or not we should therefore pray to Mary.

Jesus once said that our Father in heaven "makes His sun rise on the evil and on the good, and sends rain on the just and on the unjust" (Matthew 5:45). That tells me the Lord answers prayers of all kinds of people because He loves them, even if they are sometimes praying to the wrong god.

For the record, I believe that Mary was a saint; I believe she was the mother of Jesus, and I certainly believe in the virgin birth. But I do not find any Scripture to support that we are to pray to Mary. If you use the argument that someone prayed to Mary and received an answered prayer, then what about people who pray to cats or cockroaches and fully believe their prayers were answered? I am convicted that it is the Bible that should dictate to *whom* we give worship and direct our prayers.

The Scriptures are clear on this point. In fact, the very beginning of God's Ten Commandments states: "You shall have no other gods before Me" (Exodus 20:3). Worshiping Mary places her in a position equal with God and violates the first commandment.

Moreover, to claim that Mary is sinless denies the Scripture that "all have sinned and fall short of the glory of God" (Romans 3:23). It is also problematic to pray to Mary because of what the Bible teaches about death. "For the living know that they will die; but the dead know nothing" (Ecclesiastes 9:5). As far as we know, Mary is in the grave waiting for the resurrection.

So the best way to honor Mary is to follow her instructions to obey Jesus: "Whatever He says to you, do it" (John 2:5).

GOD'S HEALING

Does God heal people today as He did in Bible times?

"Jesus went about all Galilee…preaching the gospel of the kingdom, and healing all kinds of sickness and all kinds of disease among the people" (Matthew 4:23).

Jesus was not just interested in teaching; He also spent a significant part of His ministry making blind eyes see, opening deaf ears, removing fevers, and even raising people from the dead. Christ cared about the physical bodies of the people to whom He ministered.

When Christ sent out His 12 disciples, the Bible says, "When He had called His twelve disciples to Him, He gave them power over unclean spirits, to cast them out, and to heal all kinds of sickness and all kinds of disease" (Matthew 10:1). The ministry of healing others was not intended only for Bible times, but for all ages.

In the early church, James, the brother of Jesus, gave us instructions on special prayer for those who are sick. "Is anyone among you sick? Let him call for the elders of the church, and let them pray over him, anointing him with oil in the name of the Lord. And the prayer of faith will save the sick, and the Lord will raise him up. And if he has committed sins, he will be forgiven" (James 5:14, 15).

There are a couple guidelines to keep in mind when we pray for the sick. First, this verse suggests that a person who asks for this anointing should search their hearts and confess all known sins. Second, when we pray for healing, we should also follow Jesus' example of stating, "Your will be done" (Luke 11:2; 22:42). Sometimes people are laid to rest in the grave; it does not necessarily indicate a lack of faith. (Think of what happened to John the Baptist.) Yet a person can sincerely know that someday, at the resurrection, God will certainly "raise" them up.

Finally, we should be cautious about so-called "faith healers." There have been many examples of bogus healings where people were set up to "pretend" to be ill by a religious leader, and then later acted as if they were healed. Even Satan can delude people with healing tricks (Revelation 16:14).

CHRISTMAS TREES

Is there anything wrong with having a Christmas tree?

"She brought forth her firstborn Son, and wrapped Him in swaddling cloths, and laid Him in a manger" (Luke 2:7).

There's little reason to believe that Jesus was actually born on December 25; instead, He was probably born in the fall. One reason is that Augustus Caesar would not have required people to travel for a census during the middle of winter. Second, shepherds wouldn't have been out in the fields in late December because the climate was too cold. Third, we know Jesus' birthday was around the time of His baptism (Luke 3:23), that He ministered 3-1/2 years and died during Passover. Subtract 3-1/2 years from the springtime when He died and you come to the fall. (No one knows the exact date.)

The significance of December 25 comes from ancient cultures of the Northern Hemisphere that noticed the days getting shorter up until December 21 and then getting longer again about December 25. They called it the New Birth of the Day, among many other names. The origins for the day are rooted in astronomy more than Christianity.

Just because something has a pagan connection doesn't automatically make it wrong for a Christian; it's only wrong if it violates a Christian principle. There's no violation of a Christian principle in commemorating the birth of Christ. However, there's no command to do it either. If a person's conscience bothers them, they can freely choose not to celebrate the birth of Jesus.

Jeremiah 10:3–5, which talks about carving idols from a tree, has no connection to Christmas trees as we know them. The Christmas tree comes from a tradition in Scandinavian countries; they would cut down and decorate a tree. An evergreen tree doesn't lose its leaves, and that supposedly represents an enduring life.

There's also nothing wrong with exchanging gifts or giving gifts to the Lord. "It is more blessed to give than to receive" (Acts 20:35). Of course, if you're spending yourself into oblivion or only thinking about what gifts you're going to get, that's a poor spirit—but Christmastime can actually be a good opportunity for believers to witness about Jesus.

HOMOSEXUALITY

Is homosexuality a sin?

"Do you not know that the unrighteous will not inherit the kingdom of God? Do not be deceived. Neither fornicators, nor idolaters, nor adulterers, nor homosexuals, nor sodomites" *(1 Corinthians 6:9).*

The Bible makes clear statements about the practice of homosexuality. The apostle Paul writes, "For this reason God gave them up to vile passions. For even their women exchanged the natural use for what is against nature. Likewise also the men, leaving the natural use of the woman, burned in their lust for one another, men with men committing what is shameful, and receiving in themselves the penalty of their error which was due" (Romans 1:26, 27).

In the Old Testament, we find laws about practicing homosexual behavior. "You shall not lie with a male as with a woman. It is an abomination" (Leviticus 18:22). The Bible outlines many sexual perversions and teaches that the only pure sexual relationship is between a husband and a wife. All else is a form of adultery.

There are two important points that get lost in the discussion about homosexuality. First, the Bible does not condemn people for having same-sex attractions, but it does condemn the act of homosexual behavior. Being tempted is not sin, but acting on that temptation is sin. Like any other sinful behavior, the Lord asks us to repent and promises to forgive us.

This leads to a final point. There is hope for the person practicing homosexual behavior. God promises to give us power to stop all sinful actions. In 1 Corinthians 6:9, Paul describes different types of sinful activities, including homosexuality. He then states, "Such were some of you. But you were washed, but you were sanctified, but you were justified in the name of the Lord Jesus and by the Spirit of our God" (1 Corinthians 6:11).

We should treat all people with respect and kindness, regardless of their sexual orientation. At the same time, we can remember, "No temptation has overtaken you except such as is common to man; but God is faithful, who will not allow you to be tempted beyond what you are able, but with the temptation will also make the way of escape, that you may be able to bear it" (1 Corinthians 10:13).

FORNICATION

Does the Bible really speak against sex before marriage?

"Have you not read that He who made them at the beginning 'made them male and female,' and said, 'For this reason a man shall leave his father and mother and be joined to his wife, and the two shall become one flesh'?" (Matthew 19:4, 5).

It has always been God's plan that the gift of sexual intimacy be experienced only within the protective confines of a marital union. Jesus quotes from Genesis 2:24 to support that the sexual act, described as becoming "one flesh," is only to be shared between a husband and wife.

There is always an effort to rationalize away Bible truth and look for loopholes, often by young people pressuring their significant others into having pre-marital sex. But defining love by flowing hormones is anything but true love. There is no physical human act more intimate and personal than sex; the bond that is developed from this act of marriage is never meant to be broken.

The Bible teaches, "Marriage is honorable among all, and the bed undefiled; but fornicators and adulterers God will judge" (Hebrews 13:4). You defile the marriage bed by sleeping with someone who is not your spouse. The apostle Paul specifically defines such sin: "Because of sexual immorality, let each man have his own wife, and let each woman have her own husband" (1 Corinthians 7:2).

Paul becomes even more blatant in describing the act of unmarried people engaging in sex. "Or do you not know that he who is joined to a harlot is one body with her? For 'the two,' He says, 'shall become one flesh'" (1 Corinthians 6:16). Sex is like spiritual glue that connects two people, a husband and a wife. Marriage safeguards this special bond.

It is not without reason that God wants us to protect this gift. When we look at the broken hearts and bodies of people who believe in recreational sex outside the boundaries of marriage, we see people who struggle with sexually transmitted diseases, abortions, unwed mothers, unwanted pregnancies, and kids growing up with one parent. Abstinence before marriage honors life and can save us from grief.

INTERRACIAL MARRIAGE

Does the Bible speak against interracial marriages?

"There is neither Greek, nor Jew, circumcised, barbarian, Scythian, slave nor free, but Christ is all and in all" (Colossians 3:11).

There is only one incident in the Bible that directly addresses the issue of interracial marriage, and that took place when Miriam and Aaron criticized their brother Moses "because of the Ethiopian woman whom he had married" (Numbers 12:1). As a consequence, Miriam became leprous, "as white as snow" (v. 10). Even though she sinned against her brother, Moses pleaded with God to heal his sister. The Lord did heal her, but only after she remained outside the camp for seven days.

There is an issue deeper than skin color or race that is addressed in finding a marital partner. The Bible says, "Do not be unequally yoked together with unbelievers. For what fellowship has righteousness with lawlessness? And what communion has light with darkness?" (2 Corinthians 6:14). Why is that important? God once told the Israelites to destroy all the people in the land of Canaan and not to intermarry with them because they will "turn your sons away from following Me, to serve other gods" (Deuteronomy 7:4).

The main factor in a successful marriage is that it is built on a common commitment to follow Jesus Christ. There is no perfect person. Someone once said marriage is not just about finding the right person, but being the right person. When both spouses look to Jesus for guidance, it will help the couple surmount any obstacle.

It is appropriate to reflect on the potential challenges people of different races might face if they choose to get married. While it's not wrong, it could be difficult. Emotional love can make us blind to potential problems. We live in an imperfect world with less than ideal neighbors and communities. Children born into marriages with mixed race parents face prejudices that are deep. This is not true everywhere, but in some societies it can create tough barriers.

What is plain from our text for today is that there is no segregation of races in God's eyes. Salvation is a free gift to all people regardless of their ethnicity.

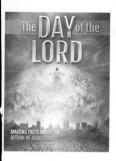

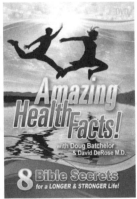